WORKING CLASS COMMUNITY

*Some general notions
raised by a series of studies
in northern England*

WORKING
CLASS
COMMUNITY

Some general notions
raised by a series of studies
in northern England

by
Brian Jackson

FREDERICK A. PRAEGER, *Publishers*
New York · Washington

BOOKS THAT MATTER

Published in the United States of America in 1968
by Frederick A. Praeger, Inc., Publishers
111 Fourth Avenue, New York, N.Y. 10003

Library of Congress Catalog Card Number: 68–25543

12558

Printed in Great Britain

CONTENTS

for
BRIAN, DOUGLAS, SHEILA

ACKNOWLEDGEMENTS

My chief debt in preparing this book is to Dennis Marsden who did so much of the early fieldwork and writing up, and in particular put far more than I did into the section on the Mill. If life had been rather different this might have been a joint book with him, and the better for it. The cost of the initial interviewing was met by the Frederick Soddy Trust who got the venture off the ground. It was saved from collapse by further help from Michael Young and the Institute of Community Studies. And that it was written up at all is due to the generosity of the Department of Applied Economics and its director W. B. Reddaway who during my time as a visiting member there gave me the space and quietness I couldn't otherwise have had.

I don't suppose I would have stuck at the project at all had I not only had initial help from Sheila Jackson with the fieldwork and writing up, but generous and selfless encouragement all the way through. Drafts of this book have been circulating for five years, and many people put long hours, sometimes at considerable personal inconvenience, into helping me with it. Perhaps I've drawn most on the help of Jeremy Mulford, David Grugeon, Peter Laslett, Sonia Abrams, Richard Hoggart, Royston Lambert, Jennifer Platt, Kim Townsend and Douglas Brown. But the crises, complications and pressures of other work have been so strong that this book has had to be fitted into odd days over the last six years, and to do all that has meant that I've leaned more heavily than I care to acknowledge on the perception and patience both of the people I mention, and many other friends and colleagues.

Chapter One

VOICES

'I got hit with a frying pan one day. When I got married and lived with my husband's mother, there was a do up our street. I was fascinated, and I got a bit too close. Old Ma Ryan threw a frying pan at her husband and I got it. My mother-in-law said it served me right for being too nosy.'

'We've been in Millbank Methodist Chapel all our lives, we've been connected but no, we never went, not after we were little you know. Bah, you had to go, it were a case of your parents making you go in them days, you had to do as you were told. What, don't you forget it, it were real in them days, but when we'd taken each other like, we didn't go no more.'

'I'll tell you what, I've noticed this with old folk that's been moved away—they don't seem to have reigned long. It's too bad rehousing old people, they should leave them alone. I'll give you an example, that woman over there, her sister and her husband they were moved from Brow Road. Well he were a big mate o' mine, used to go about a lot, and they were moved up Crosland Moor. Well nothing wrong with Crosland Moor, up top end it's a nice district, but do you know they were both dead within twelve month. Somehow it seemed to knock all t'stuffing out of them, down here you know everything and everybody, I know Millbank stone by stone as you might say.'

'I know one or two Indians. I go drinking with them, they're nice blokes. Of course since this Mau Mau job we've got something against the Jamaicans. We're not so keen on them.'

'We used to think it was real going down to Chinny's, to the dance. Getting black drainpipes on, and a long duffle coat, and you looked exactly like a bopper. I couldn't bop, but I used to think it was real, and we felt it was smashing going out with greasy faces. We just used to put Hi-Fi on, smear it all over our faces, no powder or anything and lots of black mascara. Then we'd go down in the dark and we'd feel exactly like boppers. It didn't last though, you don't stop at Chinny's very long. Then after Chinny's, you go to the Empress or Charlie Frost's. Oh I remember a time down there, the first time I ever went to Chinny's, and I wasn't wearing the right clothes or anything, I'd gone in a sort of party frock. And everybody else they all looked at me, and I cried upstairs because I couldn't get anybody to dance with me, and then somebody danced with me and I thought I'd got a partner, but it turned out it was a girl I went with, that had put him up to it. So next time I went, I got the proper clothes on, except I'd got a blouse on under me sweater and the neck was all showing you know. When I got there and took me coat off, they all looked at me and they said, you don't wear a blouse under your sweater, and they made me go upstairs and take it off straight away.'

'I always give to the blind, but I don't like these other things. What I want to know is where does all the money go? There's too many of these things. There's somebody filling their nests. Where's it go? Congo? Why, we've enough of our own refugees in England without bothering sending money to that lot. They want to get some work done, that's what they want. Like the rest of us have to do. I work with a black woman and I should know.'

'There's this guy next door, Mr. Nugent, an Irishman. When he's sober he dresses quite smart, but when he's drunk—he shouts out "Get out! Get out of my house!" And they *have* to get out. All twelve. He has twelve children. And some nights he shouts out "which is the finest race?" And they have to shout back, all in unison they have to shout back "The Irish!" Or else he might have them all saying "Heil! Heil Hitler!" When the police come, he gets out of the bathroom window.'

'On this estate you've got more community spirit than you would have, say, down Edgefield—real community. We've got to think first of all of getting this on a local scale; everybody in Huddersfield being co-operative and community-minded. Then on a national scale. Then on an international scale. I take it that's brotherhood.'

Chapter Two

STYLES OF LIVING

When you hear them, those voices are Yorkshire, deliberate, authoritative within their worlds. This book is an attempt to exemplify why they matter, why we should hear them. They are all working-class voices—the mill girl at the dance, the plumber with his vision of 'brotherhood', the labourer climbing out of the bathroom window. Following their leads, I've tried in half a dozen ways to define the qualities, good or bad, of working-class life: the styles of living that it offers us.

Listening to the voices, or exploring the communities that have gathered around the weaving sheds, I shall be asking a series of familiar questions. Questions about the clash between established working-class values and established middle class values; about those older working-class values and their encounter with the mass media; and most of all, about whether the new world of relative affluence inevitably means the total end of the old styles of living. To be extreme: are we, by a thousand and one deliberate decisions, moving in the direction of a society sapped by the poorest middle-class concerns (such as those about personal status), the poorest mass media attitudes—(those preoccupied with the packaging and not the packet's contents), and the poorest of all the old working-class situations: a vast but enclosed community transformed into a passive, conforming audience? Or can the decisions, in an inevitably changing society, be taken differently? Can they lead to a fusion of middle class feeling for individual development, with the multiplication of experience that the mass media may offer, and those qualities of spontaneity and community that my opening 'voices' suggest?

It would be a bold man who could tackle such large generalities head-on. In most of this enquiry I have explored the questions indirectly, letting the patterns establish themselves and

3

knowing that my pattern would not always be the reader's.

This study began, in 1958, out of that debate on working-class life which blazed up, and died down, so very quickly. *The Uses of Literacy* was fresh on the bookstalls, so was *Saturday Night and Sunday Morning*. On television Dennis Mitchell was showing *Morning in the Streets*. The papers were attending to the work on family and kinship that Michael Young and his colleagues were reporting from Bethnal Green. And the whole structure of our school and university system was clarified by findings of untapped working-class talent recorded in such surveys as Floud, Halsey and Martin's *Social Class and Educational Opportunity*. Looking back, we can see that there was an element of fashion in the extent to which this debate was taken up. No doubt our society needs to discover a working-class novelist every three or four years as a kind of exotic thrill: it needs the sense of a rough, sexy, warm, violent world just around the corner. The nineteenth century was in the habit of taking up a working-class poet every few years— John Clare is a sad example. But the subsequent discussions on rural strengths and uncomplicated freshness of response, though they concerned real qualities (for Clare is still alive and his lionizers dead), were often part of the froth of intellectual diversion. Something like this happened around 1958.

But of course the questions raised at the time remain important and unanswered, and people have continued the work. Any 'answering' must be a collaborative activity involving not only many people, but time itself and the insight of several disciplines. These are not questions for the sociologist or the psychologist or the literary critic or the writer or the film producer alone; but for all of them on our behalf.

The ground work was laid in the previous debate. For the matters I intend to explore here, the most interesting survey was *Family and Kinship in East London*.[1] In this Michael Young and Peter Willmott analysed the way the working-class family centred on Mum: daughters married and lived close by, and the 'extended family' stretched over several households. Most of their report suggested strengths in this system, especially for the women: there was abundant mutual help—looking after children, cooking

[1] Young, M. and Willmott, P. *Family and Kinship in East London* (Routledge and Kegan Paul, 1957).

meals, sharing shopping. There was quick support in the great personal crises of death, accident and illness, and a constant flow of more everyday advice and encouragement. The 'extended family' mattered a great deal too for men and women—a widow, an unmarried son—who might otherwise live isolated lives in small flats. In East London they were absorbed into the linked system of households, often taking on satisfying roles as substitute sons or mothers. Against this, the authors contrasted an analysis of a new housing estate where material conditions were vastly superior—hot water, gardens, good schools—and where husband and wife were closer together. Nevertheless there was unhappiness and loneliness, and the loss of the 'extended family' meant that a vital part of working-class life, with much of the emotional and practical support it offered, had been needlessly destroyed. It was needless, they concluded, because housing schemes could be built round the existing style of living: to destroy that and substitute an estate with a 'community centre' was useless action based on ignorance of our own society. The importance of this survey and the others that cluster round it[1] lies firstly in their unravelling of the kinship network which underlies all working-class 'community'. Secondly, they changed the focus from untypical 'problem families' or male-centred discussions of collective bargaining and the creation of trade unions, to the ordinary world of women and home. And they show the quite needless harm that can be done by well-meaning middle-class officials and policy makers who take their decisions in ignorance of the style of living around them.

This interpretation does not go unchallenged. In *Ship Street*, a Liverpool 'problem family' study, Madeleine Kerr emphasized the restrictive and smothering role of Mum, whose emotional hold makes it difficult for the children ever to break away—even into a larger and more attractive life. And in *Coal is Our Life*,[2] an enquiry centred on Featherstone in Yorkshire, Dennis, Henriques

[1] Especially Townsend, P. *Family Life of Old People* (Routledge and Kegan Paul, 1957); Marris, P. *Widows and their Families* (Routledge and Kegan Paul, 1958); Mogey, J. M. *Family and Neighbourhood* (Clarendon Press, 1956); Bott, E. *Family and Social Network* (Tavistock Publications, 1957).

[2] Dennis, N., Henriques, P., and Slaughter, C. *Coal is Our Life* (Eyre and Spottiswoode, 1956).

and Slaughter looked at working-class life from the point of view of the men at their jobs. They showed the tightness of the historical bond between the men expressed daily in all manner of mutual help and personal generosities.

'When I was lamed five years ago, and I came out of hospital on crutches, I.J. was the first one to buy me a drink. Since then he has given me 2s. 6d. or 3s. or whatever change he has happened to have in his pocket, so that I could have a quiet drink.

'I can't pay him back straight away. But I had a pair of glasses and I.J. tried them on. "Champion! Just right!" he said.

' "Put them in your pocket," I said.

' "What do you want for them?" he said (i.e. how much do you want to sell them for?).

' "I want you to put them in your pocket, that's what I want! My eyes are too far gone for reading glasses." '

But they argued also against the shifting orthodoxy of life, and suggested that the women's life especially was one of subjection (contraceptives thrown on the fire because they took all enjoyment out of sex, husband's wages never known, violence at night when he returned with a skinful of ale). And a life too which did not allow for 'much expression of qualities of intellect or personality'. I take these different studies as being representative of the knowledge we have of the centre of working-class community, the family. Since 1958 the drift of evidence has largely been behind the first account—that the 'extended family' makes good sense, and helps many millions of people to lead humdrum but satisfying lives. The other picture—violence, sexual aggression and ignorance, small narrow lives—flares up less frequently. It has authority behind it, yet it no longer—except in lighter fiction—can be offered as the typical account.

But at this point the enquiry into community slowed down. Instead, interest and research split into several channels. Much the most successful—they were with the tide—were those enquiries which considered the degree to which the education system failed to bring out the best in working-class children. Stimulating and underpinning a series of major government reports—*Crowther, Newsom, Robbins*—they led to a vastly enlarged sense of how much the nation needed these children to realise their gifts, especially through the universities. And working at another level they communicated the subtle relationship between a child's 'social' and 'academic' education, within what was shown to be a class system of schools, and so helped to promote the gradual growth of comprehensive education. Out of this movement will probably come a sharper penetration of the working-class community by formal education and those 'outside' experiences it brings to the individual. At the same time, though slowly and with many snags, the comprehensive school—a neighbourhood school—may help transform the existing physical community into an educational community. If so, though the line is pitted with difficulties, the sixth-form girl may no longer be writing in her library, sharply rejecting the community from which she comes for the élite she is promised.

Less successful, but often more impressive, has been that line of enquiries from Richard Titmuss' *Essays on the Welfare State*[1] to Peter Townsend's research into the situation of old people, the sick, the unemployed, the widowed, the workers on low wages with large families. These have substantially altered the common view that need and poverty ended in the 1930s, and that today the working-class is affluent and moving easily into a middle-class standard and style of living. Titmuss has often shown how the welfare services—state hospitals, free medical care, family allowances, pensions—have worked to the advantage of the middle class, and frequently widened the gaps between manual workers and others. And in a neat summary[2] of the available evidence he suggests that since the levelling period of 1940-50, there have been substantial increases in inequality. He contrasts our imperfect knowledge of middle class wealth and income with the sharp public attention given to the earnings of working-class boys and girls compared with middle class children, and comments:

'Later in life, however, the latter may be twenty times or more better off than the former, measured solely in terms of annual cash income,

[1] Titmuss, R. M., *Essays on the Welfare State* (Allen and Unwin, 1958) and such reports as Townsend, P. *The Last Refuge* (Routledge and Kegan Paul, 1962); Lynes, T. *National Assistance and National Prosperity* (Codicote Press, 1962); Townsend, P. and Wedderburn, D. *The Aged in the Welfare State* (Bell, 1965); Wedderburn, D. *Redundancy and the Railwaymen* (Cambridge University Press, 1965).

[2] Titmuss, R. M. Introduction (1964) to Tawney, R. H. *Equality*.

with less disabling disease, a longer expectation of life, a lower age of retirement, more inherited wealth, a proportionately greater and more assured pension, a tax free lump sum perhaps one hundred times greater, and in receipt of substantially more non-wage income and amenities in forms that escape income tax, being neither money nor convertible into money. Which of two individuals from these classes receives more aid in absolute terms from the generality of taxpayers through "the social services" and other redistributive mechanisms, especially during that phase of life when the foundations of earning capacity, opportunity and achievement are laid?'

Peter Townsend and those around him have broadened the great tradition—Rowntree, Booth, the Webbs—of enquiries into working-class poverty. He has shown that in 1965 there are still seven and a half million people living below an income level set by the National Assistance Board as necessary for rent, clothing and food. 'Poverty' needs to be redefined in each age: it is a relative statement of lack of primary wants.[1] It may be less visible than it was. The great city sprawls—Attercliffe in Sheffield, Stepney and Bethnal Green, the Gorbals—are not as horrifying as they were. But it still exists, on a big scale, in a complicated system of pockets —the large family at the end of the street, the widow in the basement flat. This research has given us new eyes. It has insisted that behind the 'community' problem—and behind all the fractions of it, such as education—still lie crude problems of neglect and extreme inequality: and that the solution of those is the first priority.

A third line of enquiry has concerned itself with the nature and effect of the mass media. Probably the most important achievement here of writers such as Richard Hoggart and Raymond Williams has been to break up the easy concept of the working-class 'masses' being given the rubbish they ask for and being well satisfied with it. ('Masses are other people. There are in fact no

[1] 'The children of 1965 are in some ways more deprived than the poor of the 1940s when there was a communal poverty. They are surrounded by apparent affluence. They have no vests and shoes that are too tight, but other children in their classes will be talking about the Continental holidays they are going to have. Children who go to school badly dressed are not usually spotted as being poor, unless it is known that their mothers are widowed or deserted.' Jean Stean commenting in the *Guardian* (2, Feb., 1966) on research by Peter Townsend and Brian Abel-Smith. See Townsend, P. 'The Meaning of Poverty'. *Brit. Journal of Sociology*, vol. XIII, no. 3, Sept., 1962. See also Runciman, W. G. *Relative Deprivation and Social Justice* (Routledge and Kegan Paul, 1966).

masses; there are only ways of seeing people as masses.')[1] It has been shown with some care that 'mass' audiences are made up of multiple, shifting sub-groups, that programmes or papers with equally large audiences are not viewed or read with equal intensity, and above all that we must beware of transferring a judgment about clichés and shallowness in magazines or television into one about trivial or stock responses in their audience. In 1958 it was easy for policy makers—like M.P.s—or the face-to-face decision takers—like teachers or doctors—to talk about 'the masses' and television in the same unquestioning way that the nineteenth-century bourgeoisie could talk about 'the masses' and the vote. That has gone, and if anything the run of new evidence now concentrates attention on the fact that the content of the media very often stems from producers, editors, writers, with middle class backgrounds and expensive educations. The more serious surrender to the 'packaging' values may come not from working-class teenagers but from ex-public schoolboys down from Cambridge knowingly grading their 'copy' according to the educational level of their audience.[2] But so far as questions of working-class community are concerned, what is now coming out of these enquiries is a sharper sense of discrimination *within* the mass media instead of the old black-and-white opposition between 'mass' art and the older 'minority' arts. ('School and home' said the Secretary of the National Union of Teachers 'are often cases threatened by the surrounding desert'.) What is only just beginning to be accepted is that the mass media—from Marks and Spencer to television—have penetrated working-class communities with new goods and experiences of an important kind.[3]

[1] Williams, R. *Culture and Society* (Chatto and Windus, 1958).

[2] 'A Bri-nylon fabric is advertised in a gay, carefree manner in *Woman's Own*, but in a suave, modish and expensively restrained way once it reaches the pages of *Queen*, *About Town* or *Vogue*. Advertising contributes to cultural stratification in our society'. Hall, S. and Whannel, P. *The Popular Arts* (1964) p. 415, from whom the quotation by the Teachers' Secretary (p. 21) and E. Shils (p. 380) are also taken.

[3] 'Mass Society has liberated the cognitive, appreciative, and moral capacities of individuals. Larger elements of the population have consciously learned to value the pleasures of eye, ear, taste, touch and conviviality. People make choices more freely in many spheres of life, and these choices are not necessarily made for them by tradition, authority, or scarcity'. Shils, E. *Culture for the Millions.*

To take a small example, the middle class with its background of good schooling over several generations, and its strong pull towards London, has easy access to the dramatic heritage of western civilisation. But the arrival of television into almost every home in Dewsbury, Warrington or Swindon is often the first sustained encounter with what 'drama' can offer as an entry into other experience: a leap of the imagination so common to many well-educated middle-class citizens, and so fundamental to their most serious culture, that they may be inclined to accept it as being open to all.

Lastly, that familiar line of enquiry which could once have been safely summarised as 'working-class problem studies', has undergone a most extraordinary change. (Though the older middle class attitudes about the 'problem' can still be tenaciously held.) This could be illustrated by recent work on delinquency,[1] but I want to take two studies of subjects that are more central to this book. The first is *Infant Care in an Urban Community*,[2] a survey of 700 Nottingham mothers. Compared with earlier work this is remarkable by virtue of its readiness to accept that varied styles of living might make sense in different ways, and its insistence that we must start by 'looking at real families'. When they did look at 'real families', they found that far from the majority of working-class husbands being absent all the time at the pub, the majority of them took a practical part in the care of small babies. 'At a time when he has more money in his pocket, and more leisure on which to spend it, than ever before, the head of the household chooses to sit at his own fireside, a baby on his knee and a feeding bottle in his hand.' Of course this is a picture of a changing life. The quality of family life has plainly been affected by the arrival of the forty-hour week, the husband having more energy and time to give to his family—especially at weekends. And during the day, the woman's load has been considerably lightened by the benefits of mass production—and even such humble things as the proliferation of effective cleaning materials, more easily

[1] Such as Wilkins, L. T. *Delinquent Generations* (H.M.S.O., 1961) which destroys many middle-class stereotypes of working-class delinquency and violence.

[2] Newson, J. and Newson, E. *Infant Care in an Urban Community* (Allen and Unwin, 1963).

prepared food, the practical information in women's magazines, or the myriad forms of the 'plastics revolution' are a boon that their mothers could hardly have conceived. All this helps to lead to a larger sense of possibilities, and more intimately, to a different attitude towards the small child running round the house. 'I think we're not so happy about *ourselves* these days, we blame ourselves, not the child.' Of course the middle-class mother still has the advantage. In this survey we see how her doctors automatically get her into the desired maternity hospital, whilst working-class patients must more frequently have their babies at home. And her material and educational start makes it easier for her to rear a child according to principles and not to a succession of impulses. But the Newsoms record how this has its unhappier side, how sometimes the child can be obscured by the principle. A study like this neatly recalls the liberating effects of better conditions, and yet has the virtue of 'looking at real families' and not (like most mothercraft literature and not a little social science) basing itself on unquestioned stereotypes of the working-class home.

The same spirit in what once would have been 'problem studies' can be illustrated from the work of Dr. Basil Bernstein.[1] It has been recognised since J. D. Nisbett's *Family Environment* (1953) that in large families the IQ tends to drop successively after the first child. This applies in all social classes, and is probably because the only child is surrounded by an environment of adult language during his most formative years, whilst the youngest child of six is surrounded by a less stimulating environment of 'child' language. Bernstein starting with this subtle sense of an environment ('out there') which progressively becomes part of the child's thought structure and emotional definition ('in there')—reworked the problem in terms of social class. He produces research evidence to support two suppositions. The first is that there is a kind of language (he calls it 'public') which *is* used by most working-class people as their *only* language, and *can* be used by most middle-class people when they choose. It is a style of language which is con-

[1] See Bernstein, B. 'Social Class and Linguistic Development' in Halsey) A. M., Flood, J., and Anderson, C. A., *Education, Economy and Society* (1961, and Social Class, Speech Systems and Psycho-Therapy' in *Brit. Journal of Sociology*, Vol. XV, no. 1, March 1964.)

crete and descriptive, arguing or thinking in terms of a succession of anecdotes. The second kind of language which is *only* usually used by the middle class (partly because of the generations of education and intellectually exacting experience and occupation behind them) he calls 'formal'. By this he means a manner of speech which can handle concepts, the language of ideas. Its syntax is much more complex and is so built up that even small children can immediately begin thinking in conceptual rather than descriptive ways. He quotes two four-year-old girls arguing in a middle-class home. 'I'm bigger than *you*.' 'No, I'm bigger than *you*.' 'Well, my sister's seven and a half.' 'Well, but she's not you.' 'No, everyone's theirselves.'

In a society such as that of Elizabethan England, the command of 'public' language—anecdotal, descriptive, metaphorical—could give access to the central culture of that age. But in a scientific, technological age it may well be that, as Bernstein's work suggests, 'formal' conceptual language has to be mastered if a child is to advance through education. There is an unseen breakdown of communication between working-class children and their teachers. 'The methods and problems of teaching need to be thought out almost as though middle class children do not exist. This does not imply that pupils of the two social strata need to be educated in different institutions.'

Bernstein's own thoughts are constantly changing, and one need not wholly agree with the concepts of 'public' and 'formal' language, to see that his analysis of an old 'problem' ('By fourteen years of age many lower working-class children have become "unteachable".') carries an importance outside the school system. It implies that working-class life—especially that of the semi-skilled and unskilled—is surrounded by a language barrier, and that the breakdown of communication now revealed between teacher and pupil probably exists in the same way between the working-class man or woman and all those representatives of the middle class world—doctors, matrons, magistrates, council officials—who have such a day-to-day influence on his life. It also tells us something more than we knew in 1958 about 'community' and about the working-class 'voice.' In these analyses, working-class language tends to communicate *similarities* rather than differences in experience: it reinforces feelings of solidarity.

Middle class language tends to define, in elaborate ways, the individual as against the group. There is one important qualification which, one may feel, is by no means explained. This is that working-class language can have a peculiar power of uttering direct personal experience, not only through description and anecdote as in my opening 'voices', but through image and metaphor like the great creative artists—'it hurts like my head's coming off my neck.' 'It's like broken glass inside me.' And its very lack of the abstract means that *people*, and the habit of valuing people rather than things, principles or ideas is very deeply inbred indeed.

Since the general 'debate' about working-class life around 1958, enquiry and analysis has continued more quietly and in more specialised forms. Instead of large questions being posed, the job has been broken down into more manageable fragments. This has been extraordinarily illuminating, and we now have a very much stronger sense and record of normal working-class life than our society has ever before possessed. It remains very insubstantial, but it is enough to challenge the romantic or offensive stereotypes still current. We have a sharpened sense of inequality and avoidable neglect. We know more than we did of working-class resilience and working-class gain from the impact of mass communications and mass production. We have a stronger notion of the reality and nature of 'community' and some clues as to those qualities of spontaneity found more frequently in working-class life. I think that the balance of evidence warns us that we must not overlook the continuing need for a more equal society. It reminds us that if a more equal society means an enormous extension not only of middle class material standards but middle class styles of living, then those styles need far more critical scrutiny. Finally it reaffirms the feeling that there is more to be valued in working-class life than was once thought: there are latent qualities which any civilised society might desire.

Yet beside what the sociologists have given us since 1958, we might also consider another kind of experience: that of the creative artist. Sociology is concerned with groups, and it is very hard within the present terms of the discipline even to remember the existence of those insights into individual life which cannot be trapped in fundamental assumptions about old orders or new orders of living. But the artist is able to embody perceptions of the individual life which can be disruptive, anarchic, asocial. It would be possible here to turn to those novelists or playwrights— John Braine, Arnold Wesker, Alan Sillitoe—who have since the 1950s been giving *their* kind of account of working-class life. I don't do so, because I have never been strongly moved by them. To my judgment, they have all illustrated social truths in memorable ways. But they are (perhaps it is inevitable) too close to the sociologist or the documentary reporter to offer the kind of creative experience I'm concerned with here. That, I think, can be found with authority in three artists from the industrial north— the painter L. S. Lowry, the novelist D. H. Lawrence, and the sculptor Henry Moore.

Lowry clears the eyes of prejudice. His paintings recreate grey, smoke-laden skies pierced by the black shafts and towers of mill chimneys, market halls, Victorian schools, Nonconformist chapels, soot-screened cathedrals: the institutional life of a northern city. And underneath them the long row of brick houses, the patches of derelict land, and the busy life of the street. It is hard to see Halifax or Huddersfield without eyes tutored in the images of other cities—metropolitan, country cathedral, garden suburb. With those 'ideal' pictures somewhere in our minds we see Halifax in so far as it falls short or measures up. Looking through Lowry's eyes one sees the industrial city as it essentially is, unblurred by other expectations. He uncovers its visual identity; a very formidable one. But it is the crowds—the shifting bunches of men and women—that he most poignantly embodies in successive images. Picture after picture gives us the flow of crowds: streaming out of work, gathering for the football match, ringing the speaker in the park, spreading out at the seaside, gossiping on the steps or round the corner shop. Even the children, one notes, move about in tiny processions—and everywhere the Lowry dogs, like a visual rhetoric underscoring the intense sociability of the paintings, and the need not to be left out. As the eye moves over the figures, each has its own voice and interest—the crippled woman close to the iron railings, the middle-aged man, dressed in Sunday best, lying flat on the sands, sleeping it off whilst a stray dog barks unheard three yards away. And yet they are all markedly

'Lowry' men and women: their identity is not only individual, it is very much shared: of a kind. These could never be other than paintings of working-class communities.

But they remain very lonely paintings. More lonely even than those Utrillos in which a single figure walks away from us beneath the idealised dome of Sacré Coeur. With Lowry it is as if the painting is a window view: the life is 'out there' but you are separate from it. No working-class artist could have created them: to be so clear sighted, or so self-conscious, about 'community' one has to be outside it and living a life of individual realization that the packed, public sociability of the working-class world denies. Nevertheless that life of 'individual realization' desires what, in the given situation, it cannot have—those very capacities for dense mutuality which would cramp it. The working-class debate, or rather the relationship between the debaters and their subject, is trapped there for ever.

D. H. Lawrence was born at Eastwood in Nottinghamshire, and his father was a miner who had worked at Brinsley Colliery since boyhood. 'My father loved the pit. He was hurt badly, more than once, but he would never stay away. He loved the contact, the intimacy, as men in the war loved the intense male comradeship of the dark days. They did not know what they had lost till they lost it.' Lawrence was never wholly in that community of men, nor the daytime community of women, children and the old. His mother felt she had married beneath her and yearned that education should lift her boys out of this colliery life. Lawrence is, I suppose, a classic example of the 'scholarship boy', but is very much more than that. To discuss his achievement in a brief paragraph or so, and only in terms of its insights into working-class life is enormously to reduce it. But within this fraction of his talent he was able—in *Sons and Lovers, The Rainbow, Daughters of the Vicar, Nottingham and the Mining Country*—both to recreate the communities of class, and yet to stand outside them. No one can more vitally communicate the intimacy of working-class life, and few can more sharply judge its limitations: 'the working-class is narrow in outlook, in prejudice. . . . This again makes a prison'. His most marvellous insights are into the bonds of men at work together, into the centrality of the mother and the home, and into the searing moments of exclusion.

' "He's here. Where is he? Morel's lad?"

'The fat, red, bald little man peered round with keen eyes. He pointed at the fireplace. The colliers looked round, moved aside, and disclosed the boy.

' "Here he is!" said Mr. Winterbottom.

'Paul went to the counter.

' "Seventeen pounds eleven and fivepence. Why don't you shout up when you're called?" said Mr. Braithwaite. He banged on to the invoice a five-pound bag of silver, then in a delicate and pretty movement, picked up a little ten-pound column of gold, and plumped it beside the silver. The gold slid in a bright stream over the paper. The cashier finished counting off the money; the boy dragged the whole down the counter to Mr. Winterbottom, to whom the stoppages for rent and tools must be paid. Here he suffered again.

' "Sixteen an' six," said Mr. Winterbottom.

'The lad was too much upset to count. He pushed forward some loose silver and half a sovereign.

' "How much do you think you've given me?" asked Mr. Winterbottom.

'The boy looked at him, but said nothing. He had not the faintest notion.

' "Haven't you got a tongue in your head?"

'Paul bit his lip, and pushed forward some more silver.

' "Don't they teach you to count at the Board-school?" he asked.

' "Nowt but algibbra an' French," said a collier.

' "An' cheek an' impidence," said another.

'Paul was keeping someone waiting. With trembling fingers he got his money into the bag and slid out. He suffered the tortures of the damned on these occasions.

'His relief, when he got outside, and was walking along the Mansfield Road, was infinite.'

But Lawrence's distinction does not only lie there—in being able to recreate in vibrant prose that feeling not of a window on working-class community, but of being within and yet not wholly of it. Lawrence goes further, for his perceptions into forms of middle-class life are no less central: 'the middle class . . . I admit them charming and educated and good people often enough. But they just stop some part of me from working.' He is able to go beyond any position that a sociologist could reach: he records the problem of loss—'class makes a gulf across which all the best human flow is lost'—but does more than balance one class against another. By virtue of his extraordinary genius he wins us 'entry into the finer, more vivid circle of life', apprehending both the intense presence of the natural world and the subtle flux of human feelings within it. So that one comes to feel that large though his realization of individual life is, it could only have been nurtured by those earlier experiences and recreations of direct and communal living in Eastwood. Aldous Huxley wrote of him in his diary of 1927 'Of most other eminent people I have met I feel that at any rate I belong to the same species as they do. But this man has something different and superior in kind, not degree.' And later he added 'To be with Lawrence was a kind of adventure, a voyage of discovery into newness and otherness. . . . He seemed to know, by personal experience, what it was like to be a tree or a daisy or a breaking wave or even the mysterious moon itself.' The fulness of life rendered in his best novels and tales goes beyond not only the 'social' but beyond the 'individual' too. The experience he discovered and offers are not a matter of 'communal' life or 'individual' life: it is larger than the first and more unique than the second, but it grows from a perception of individual life which yet knows and values that part of itself which can only exist in terms of larger community. Until we produce a greater artist, Lawrence reminds us of the final placing of any considerations of community and personal identity.

Henry Moore was born in Castleford, a small Yorkshire mining town a few miles away from Huddersfield, and close to Feather-stone, the township reported in *Coal is Our Life*. Moore's father was a collier, until he was injured in a pit accident—and as a boy the young sculptor was often aware of the buzz of trade union meetings in the front room of their terrace house. As with Lawrence, there were strong educational aspirations in the home, and Moore's first move away from the community came with his entry to Castleford Grammar School. But he was a 'scholarship boy' who was able to grow powerfully from and out of that community, rather than one who had to reject part of it in order to discover himself. 'It would be a mistake to regard such a physical environment as in any sense frustrating to a boy like Henry. . . . He himself now declares that he would not change his childhood for any other that he can imagine—certainly not for the childhood of the boys of the upper classes who were sent away to public schools and never experienced the rich communal life of the streets.'[1] The close physical life—the miner washing in front of the fire, the small houses, the crowded communal life—bred their own strange results. 'His mother suffered from rheumatism . . . and when Henry was old enough and strong enough she would ask him to rub her back with the strong-smelling liniment she herself made. The liniment smarted and brought tears to his eyes, but what was to endure all his life was the physical sensation conveyed by his fingers as they came in contact with the bones beneath the flesh.' The packed life, physical immediacy, the centrality of the mother: one begins to see how, given extraordinary talent, such a community could help foster the artist who gave us those wartime *Shelter Drawings*. In page after page of these marvellous sketches we feel the tube shelters crowded with sleeping Londoners, and in sleep—all the distinguishing marks of identity muted—you feel what is shared rather than separate, what is mutual (all of those reaching, clasping arms) within uniqueness. At that moment of extreme danger—nights in the London blitz—the metropolitan entertained for a while that sense and action of community with which this discussion is concerned. But to limit Moore to this is to curtail his genius. In growing from his community into his own kind of being, he did not take on another social identity. His stormy years at the Royal College attest that his freedom from working-class life involved no acceptance of the styles of middle class life he encountered. As with Lawrence, his penetration lies the opposite way. He brings to the great European tradition of madonna and child studies, his own original impulses: the reclining woman, the woman with child, and the long struggle to draw in the man and fuse him in the created vision of the family group. And more than that, those restless variations on the theme of the reclining woman or family grouping (searching, in his own words, for the image 'giving out something of the energy and power of great mountains') become more than representative of the human. They are at the same time analogues of the terrestrial landscape, plateau, gulf, and peak, eroded and wind-shaped: and always containing the holes and caverns from which life issues and returns. They are representative not only of human life, but of all life and of the physical

[1] Read, H. *Henry Moore* (Thames and Hudson, 1965).

18

dimension in which it exists. There is nothing in this of 'social class': we would not otherwise be moved by its universality. But what *is* interesting and important from the point of view of the social conditions which bred Moore, is that they contained values and experiences which he was able to write large and transform: that they fostered, not curtailed his extraordinary growth, and that embryonic qualities in the life he knew could, through his genius, attain to images common to all men.

I've taken three artists who have stood in particular relationships with parts of the working-class community of the north. No doubt I could have taken others. But all three have gone far beyond the documentary, and all three are *felt* artists of our age, part of our pattern of responses. What they have to tell us cannot be read in the same ways as that of the sociologists. Their evidence is much more subtle, and its roots run deeper. To no small extent our sense of what life and its values is, derives from the artist. We ought at least to pause over the community that differently stimulated all three.

So far then, I've summarised the knowledge that social science has given us over the last few years. And I've noted that there are kinds of knowledge which we do have access to—that from the artists—which we might be tempted to overlook since it may not be containable within the academic disciplines on which we mainly take our stand. From time to time the larger question about working-class community—its nature, resilience, and potential contribution to a future society—attracts general interest. This happened strikingly around 1958. Since then considerable gains have been won, but in separate ways. Sufficient, I think, to make the old questions worth re-examining.

Before doing that I shall look at community in a different way. The following chapters accept what has been summarised as 'read', in that they cannot claim to be another family and neighbourhood study. They are concerned to explore 'community' and its voices outside the family circle: to look at that mesh of groups which lie between the intimate world of home and kin and the national world of those big movements—trade unions, the co-ops, chapel, football—which stem so largely from working-class communities. All the studies are concerned with life in and near Huddersfield. The final one considers what this suggests for the notions under discussion, what we know of working-class life, what we inevitably must lose, and what we could, if we chose, retain and rework.

Huddersfield

All the evidence here is drawn from Hudderfield in the West Riding of Yorkshire. It has a population of 130,000. Its main industries are textiles and engineering, but it has such a wide spread of employment that it has seldom been liable to serious unemployment. A few miles away are Leeds, Bradford, Halifax, Wakefield, Sheffield. Between them lie great stretches of wild moorland. When John Wesley arrived here in 1757 he noted that 'A wilder people I never saw in England.' This was the beginning of the industrial revolution, and in its birth throes Huddersfield was the scene of many Luddite conspiracies, loom smashings and armed attacks on the mill owners. In its valley, Huddersfield now presents a star-shaped cluster of grimy Methodist chapels, warehouses, factories. You remember it partly because of the slender black chimneys of mill owners competing in height as they competed in trade. It has a large Irish population and you occasionally might hear Yorkshire children counting hopscotch squares on the pavement in excellent Irish. After the war Huddersfield absorbed a good number of Poles and Ukrainians. It has now taken in 7,000 immigrants from the West Indies and Pakistan, attracted by its continued work and wealth.

The place to see it from is the moorland escarpments above, from where you pick out the older Huddersfield of the canal age, and the older one still of sheep and rough cow pasture. The best time is dusk when the chains of yellow lights light up in active succession, like compass lines along the valley roads. At that moment, the canal reflections, the intense blackness of the chapels and chimneys give the town an unforgettable and unexpected Gothic beauty.

Chapter Three

BRASS BANDS

Written with Dennis Marsden

The first thing they tell you is that this is the Brass Band *Movement*. Within fifteen miles there are thirty-six bands, mostly centred in the mill villages and townships, and dating from Victorian times. Technical improvements at that time made playing much easier than before. By the turn of the century brass bands existed in thousands. Sometimes after a pint or two on a Saturday the old tag still floats back: 'sink a pit and tha starts a band, as they used to say.'

One way to meet the movement is to turn up for Sunday morning rehearsal in the bandrooms. Outside there were ten cars, four motorbikes and a tangle of cycles. Inside twenty players were blasting their way through rehearsal. Facing them were a dozen seats covered with instrument cases.

The players sat in 'contest position', cornets on one side of the conductor, trombones on the other. All were men. The oldest were 40, dressed in dark Sunday suits, and playing tubas, trombone and bugle horn. On the other side the leading cornet was 25, sporting current 'pop' clothes—tight trews, fancy waistcoat, Roman haircut. The second cornetist was 17, smiling all the time, and wearing 'pop' clothes of six months before—striped socks, thick-heeled Italian shoes, short jacket, sleek hair.

'Nah then, you're sitting there like Christmas puddings, you cornets.' The conductor stopped the music. He took the passage over again, and once more stopped.

> 'Come *on*, we want you playing like Morris Murphy. Sound every note the same, not like that cornet player at Brighouse, he's not much good.'

They start again, play for two minutes, and again are stopped. Each section is played over and over. The conductor runs one hand through his hair, and explains why he wants the crescendo on *this* note, not that, how to keep the beat in, how to negotiate a long passage of notes of equal length. Sometimes he picks out one player, and rehearses him alone for five minutes. His instructions spraddle out into lecturettes, a criss-cross of exhortation, and preaching:

'You can play it, but don't *just* play it. Always worry about something. Get the beat *right*, get *all* the notes in. Never just sit back—always *make music*. Worry. Worry about *something*. You'll never force your way past these other bands unless you do.'

An old bandsman of 70, smartly dressed, comes in, sits down and listens. Twenty minutes later he briefly interrupts progress with a loud *Good Morning*, and leaves. The band replies *Good morning*, as a body, and again blast their phrase by phrase progress. Just before one o'clock, practice stops. The Band Secretary had slipped in and sat down. Now he comes to the front and reports a letter from 'the contest'. Apparently, each band at 'the contest' has to play a twenty-minute programme, including one set 'test piece' and two of their own choice. Some grumble:

'They're getting a concert for nowt. We got paid at Blackpool for doing less 'n that.'

There is an indecisive argument about whether the band could 'borrow' four players from another band for the contest, and so rehearsal ends.

Clubmen and Idealists

A band like this has been meeting for over 100 years. There are few written records, and oral traditions are weak: the origins of these bands lie a generation or two outside living memory. There are a few recollections of the bands as 'protest' music, celebrating political defiance.

'Ah should think we're the oldest club but Ah haven't talked about it much with anybody. We played for that chap that were always against child labour in t'factories. What were his name? Eeh, Ah have it on me tongue, but Ah can't spit it out. It weren't Gaunt, what were it? Anyway this chap were flung in jail down in London, but a few of his friends got together to get him out of it, and when he came back to Huddersfield, our band met him at the station and played in front of t'procession down to t'Town Hall. Castler! that were his name.'

Yet the bands are not a dissentient movement. The fate of a 'Socialist' band in Huddersfield illustrates how the movement could not be political in its own right, though occasionally—at moments of crisis—involved with other organisations, in unity against the ruling class. One casual afternoon during the Depression the Socialist Band was founded:

'It were just one or two old men sitting about in the club and got talking and one of them said well I'll put to, and he put three half-pence down, and another put a penny down, and so on, and that was how it started. Just with coppers at beginning, but they had a good committee, and the lady members they got going and got some funds, I can remember, I was selling chocolate at work. I'd just started work then, and we used to take boxes of chocolate to work, and they were penny bars then, and I'd be selling those for the band, and then we used to have teas and whist drives.'

But the band never did well financially for several reasons:

'The trouble was with that band, we couldn't get any subscriptions from people who were better off. We had to be supported entirely by working men, and we couldn't get the players either. There were a lot of players who said to me, they said, we'd like to be in your band, we'll come and join if it wasn't for the name. It was the Socialists that put them off, you see. They didn't want to be branded as Socialists.'

Another man said,

'They used to have a rough time of it, that band. I think that's about the only political band they've ever heard of. They used to get stoned when they marched through the streets. For showing their colours like. I mean it was a big thing in those days to nail your colours to the mast.'

So the bands were supported by ordinary workmen players who were not of the stuff of political martyrs, and often patronised— gifts of money or instruments—by employers and local middle class.

Much more prominent in the band 'atmosphere' was the religious background. Some bands had been founded in Sunday Schools or chapels, only to break away from their parent bodies, long ago. Many were originally part of the anti-drink movement, and still keep their old name: Rushden Temperance, Wingates

Temperance, Pemberton Total Abstinence. The most successful band in the Huddersfield area—Brighouse and Rastrick—was originally a temperance band. It now claims to be Britain's champion 'public subscription' as opposed to 'works financed' band. Within the memory of older bandsmen, its players had to be cautious in demeanour, and at all costs avoid being seen in pubs wearing band uniform.

A more vital religious influence, which persists to the present day, is not one to be inferred from band names. The leaders of the Salvation Army early saw the values and simplicity of brass bands as an attraction for crowds and support for singing. The Salvation Army bands do not normally compete in local and national championships, but they attract and train people who pass to other, secular bands (and some of their members play in contests for other bands). One of the great prize-winning bands of recent years owes its existence to the patronage of a Salvation Army industrialist: and another Salvation Army member is one of the very few nationally famous personalities of the brass band world: Eric Ball—a prolific composer, energetic adjudicator and publicist.

Recently an advertising agency launched a campaign for one of its brewery clients. The main item was a striking picture pasted on hoardings, inserted in newspapers, encased in ash trays, etched on beer mats. It showed a huge red-faced bandsman ending a sweating round on his trombone by downing a long pint of their client's beer.

This enraged bandsmen. It was like some obscene caricature unexpectedly staring at them from the billboards. To them, this artificial, merry boozer was a gigantic alcoholic, smashing up the true image of the movement and throning himself in the public mind overnight. Their own image is not unfairly represented by the tone of their weekly magazine:

'Apart from the sheer joy of playing together, and sometimes giving valued service to the community, bandsmen receive and expect no reward, either of fame or money.

'They may not always measure up to such high musical standards as we or they would desire, although sometimes they will surprise themselves by what they can achieve; but we should all be the poorer without them, particularly because any sincere attempt to apprehend the good, the beautiful, the true, leaves a trace in life which helps mankind on an upward journey.'

The brass bandsman in Huddersfield is an idealist. To talk about the movement with him is to embark on a moral dialogue, and again and again the phrase that comes into his conversation is 'to make better music, to make music better'. In bandroom after bandroom the same warm Puritan spirit peeps through:

'Well, what always inspired me is that you have twenty-four men sweating and straining away, and for nothing. They don't get any money out of it. It's just *to make music better*. It's a movement. You can go along to a bandroom anywhere, and if you're a player, they'll soon find you an instrument, and let you have a blow with them. And if you're on your holidays, just find out where there's a band playing and go round and you've got friends. Lots of community spirit.'

It is all the more curious to hear this strain when you know that, in fact, many players do make the odd pound out of it, and those in the big works bands are essentially professionals. And it is hard to know in what sense the movement is a community. On a closer look, the band idealist stands apart from his fellow workmen. It wouldn't be so hard to pick out Mr. Ramsden at his factory bench:

'In the workshop this morning, it came out over the radio: *Music While you Work*. It was a brass band for a change. Well normally I'd have just gone on working—I'd have listened a bit if it were jazz or dance music, but I'd have gone on what I was doing. Only this time I stopped and listened. I stopped.'

And Mr. Earnshaw, though he stands with 'us' against 'them', is easily distinguishable from other factory men.

'There's this Arts Council. They're supporting ballet and opera. There's a bit of snobbery about that—not giving us any money. And then you see the BBC, they're just as bad. How much brass band music do you have on the wireless in a week? You'd be lucky if you get four half-hours—and some of it is ridiculous. Half-past six in the morning! Who wants to get up and listen then? I've tried it once or twice when I've come off nights. But you haven't really the same interest at that time of morning.'

The first big division in the movement is between the idealists, like Mr. Earnshaw, and the clubmen, who look on the club as if it were any working men's club—but with a brass band rather than a billiard team or fine concert programme as its special feature. Brass bands have traditionally played at galas, on children's treats, old folks' outings, Sunday School processions. With the coming of television, better transport, and changing domestic life, this ceremonial and public working-class life decreases. But it is still very substantial, and most of it generates not from the chapels or the unions, but from the working men's clubs. Sometimes, as at Bradley Working Men's Club, the brass bands practise in the cellar by the barrels. If this were the normal relationship then perhaps the bands would have many more members. But it is not. Of all institutions in Huddersfield working-class life, the club is the centre. But to the puritan strain of the idealists, clubs are not on the road to making music better. Most bands therefore merely have bandrooms. Those attached to clubs breed conflict.

The working men's clubs, with their prolific activities, focus and generate a community. The political groups and chapels and churches slice away a separate, gifted group of their own, but often lack dense local connections. The bands are betwixt and between.

Linkmen: the Committee Meets

In order to give the bands the structure of a movement there have to be the linkmen. These are the men (and just occasionally, women), who become secretary, treasurer, president and committee. Most of them do not play instruments, and most have held office on the committees of diverse and even clashing organisations—galas, carnivals, friendly societies, working men's clubs, Labour, Liberal and Conservative clubs, bowling, billiards, church and chapel. These men interlock the complex variety of formal organisations in working-class Huddersfield. The same faces appear round different tables, proposing motions, raising points of order and precedent, reporting profit and loss, embroiled in the common detail of insistent democracy.

One cold Tuesday evening in late January, the committee of the Huddersfield Association met in the Plough Inn. The Association represents all the Huddersfield brass bands, except for the

annual number of those who had 'disappeared' through breakdown in the structure, trouble in the band, or annoyance at the
Association's decisions.

The first linkmen settled into a small side room with a blazing
fire next to the bar. The Secretary bustled round, covering the
tables with minutes and balance sheets hoping to 'take over' the
room and deceive the landlord into expecting a large meeting.
Early arrivals bought token halves of mild. All to no purpose.
Five minutes before the meeting started they were moved to an
upstairs room, bleak and inhospitable, a new fire flickering in the
grate. Ten more members arrived and settled quietly in the long
formal U of chairs. The Secretary, busy redistributing minutes
and accounts, spoke to everyone and no one.

> 'T'landlord won't have it. That's why Ah were trying to get as
> many in as possible. Good fire. You'd think it'd be in his own
> interest. We'd be nearer t'bar, and some would have supped. They
> won't sell owt up here.'

The same room was sometimes hired out to the Jazz Club.
Crude charcoal drawings of trombonists and clarinetists marked
the walls. Quietness, except for the hiss of the damp coal and a
few whispers.

Then Mrs. Shaw, the President, arrived with five men. The
only woman of any prominence in the brass bands, she dominated
her suspicious committees:

'Come on, let's get a bit closer together.' She began fragmenting
the stiff circuit of chairs. Others clumsily rose, as seats to right
and left disappeared. Mrs. Shaw assumed the presidential chair,
letting the committee finish the job. 'Now then, let's begin.'

The meeting started ten minutes late. Minutes were read efficiently; formal with proposers, seconders, votes. The Secretary
began his report. There was nothing to report, he said. He'd
enjoyed working for the movement, enjoyed every minute of it.
But he would have to give it up this time. Not because of anything wrong in the movement; only he'd changed his job, and
the new one meant overtime in the mill. He apologised for an
item of £14 10s. od. for stationery. Stationery was very expensive.
He was very sorry. It was surprising how much stationery was
needed. He apologised for having run up such a bill. But

stationery *did* cost a lot. 'There's no need for t'secretary to apologise for money spent on letters,' said a voice.

The Secretary began his apologies again, but was overtalked: 'There's no need for any mention. Anybody who's had it to do, knows how much it costs.' The speaker was Eric Rowbottom, a mill worker, in his early sixties, frequently seen as a quiet adjudicator in local contests.

Then the Treasurer's report. A complicated business. Last year the auditor signed 'with reluctance'. This year he'd refused to touch the accounts. Most of the difficulties came from the cheques paid to member bands. Often the local band secretary didn't try to cash them until six months, even a year later. They were being treated as banknotes, and stored away in a tin box at home. More difficulties came from banking with the Co-op. The Association had had to wait whilst the Huddersfield branch office contacted Leeds, who didn't reply till they'd contacted 'London'. It was decided to leave the Co-op.

During these reports more committee men had arrived. One brought his wife, another brought his son. Despite the weak fire, the meeting took on something like a family atmosphere. Officers were elected: most posts were refused once or twice, and when accepted there were many disclaimers.

'All right, Ah'll tek it on, but Ah'll get me cards when Ah get home. When Ah were band secretary it took me all Sunday afternoon and evening to sort t'band affairs out. It's not t'job—it's what with working overtime and suchlike—Ah could do t'job just like tearing paper.'

Most of the committee men were fifty- or sixty-year-old manual workers. But in the chairs farthest away from Chairman and President were a silent group of younger men in their late twenties and early thirties. They voted together against all changes. The discussion swung against them.

'Ah do wish some o' the younger end would have a bash. Me and the other senior officers would offer every assistance. If some of the younger end would give us a bit more support, we'd be able to make this an even finer movement.'

The attack was deflected by a suggestion for a youth band.

'Aye, that's a good idea. If t'Corporation music teacher would help, there might be a chance of tapping y'town vaults there.'

There was a strong feeling that local education officials lavishly encouraged orchestral playing in schools, but weren't prepared to use school time if it was 'just for brass band stuff'. Some claimed that schools did all they could to stop young musicians going into the movement. Some, that heads and suchlike didn't really know the movement existed.

Again discussion was deflected by a stray comment:

'Shouldn't we have some players on t'committee, Madam President? Just in case of discontent, y'know. Ah don't say there *is*, but players might get talking and say: "Those block-heads who're managing this, who do they think they are?" '

'No, no. You can't do both things at once. You've got to be either a player or an organiser.'

'Ah'm not a bandsman, Ah don't play an instrument. But my reply is: "Ah'm not a hen, but Ah know an egg when Ah see one. And some of the eggs Ah've seen recently have been addled." '

Discussion shifted back to finance: a proposal to increase the levy on member bands by five shillings. In the band world money was always tight, and in this committee men talked in shillings. On other nights, at the working men's clubs, some of the same men would talk in thousands, and tens of thousands.

Then the President: a long, confident speech, overpowering the men.

'We want Huddersfield to lead the way in this country. It *does* lead the way. Mr. Barwood can verify this. When we go to meetings of the Yorkshire Association, other bands look to us to show them how to do things. But the people of Huddersfield don't know that. They're so taken up with their choirs and orchestras that they can't see what's going on in the brass band world. The only way to get that interest is to rally round the functions that we provide in the Town Hall. I know some people have supported very well. One band sent me a coachload, and others sent nobody. We made £40 on the last one. I'm coming to what I've done with the money later. I've heard some people say "Aye, she's making a good thing out o' yond". I've heard it!'

The meeting ended abruptly at ten o'clock with committee men putting on coats and rushing for the last buses. 'Not like the fratch we had last year,' said the President.

The Triumph of the Contestmen

One Saturday afternoon three months later Briggshill Silver Prize Band held a 'Slow Melody' contest in its bandrooms. The evening session began with the euphonium contest. Two men from Lockwood came on the platform. The first, aged about thirty, tall, lean, very intense, was the bandmaster. The second carried the euphonium. They sat side by side on chairs with the euphonium in between. The bandmaster counted audibly into the euphonium player's ear, making slow shovelling motions with his hands. The actual music, a heavy waltz rhythm, was trite. But the audience listened with closed eyes, beating time with fingers or conducting quietly with one hand.

This was a meeting of the contestmen. And more than clubmen, idealists or linkmen, the contestmen have carried the day, and rule the movement from within—in a more radical and all-persuasive way than the strong president. Contests began in the nineteenth century: a mill owner gladly subsidised his works band in order to do down a rival mill owner's band. But it is probably only in recent decades that the contestmen have triumphed over the idealists. Contesting has altered the whole movement, quite as radically as the introduction of beer altered the working men's clubs.

There are large numbers of local contests between band and band, or quartet contests, or slow melody contests, or contests on individual instruments—like the euphonium player and his conductor. The full band contests build up through a series of district and regional competitions into the national championships at Belle Vue, Manchester or Wembley. The first effect that the contestmen have had is to alter the music—especially over the last two decades.

Brass band music is limited in repertoire. Partly because it is handed on from generation to generation, like oral verse. There has always been a shortage of sheet music. At any meeting you hear the familiar tunes of popular religion—'Bless This House', 'Abide with Me'. In the park on a Sunday afternoon or on the Whit Walks there will be 'Colonel Bogey' and 'Senator'. But far more of the music that bandsmen play has been transcribed from oratorios ('Judas Maccabeus') or from nineteenth-century opera

('Aida', 'Carmen'). This was always the staple fare, but it is now rivalled by pieces specially composed for brass bands by leading conductors and adjudicators.

Operatic pieces have the wider appeal. They hold an audience not solely composed of brass band enthusiasts, and offer a kind of music not easily available to working men in other ways: TV for example, tends to give them either 'pop' or full-blown orchestral pieces. Brass bands playing operatic arrangements—like the song repertoire of working men's clubs—allow the audience a middle music that in some form they want, yet which 'They' do not provide. But in the hands of the contestmen curious changes occur to operatic music. In competitions the interest moves away from the generalised 'religious' sentiment of much working men's music, to matters of technique, performance, presentation. For example:

> 'That contest at Wigan was the worst run I've ever been to. Last time, we played a piece by Verdi. Well it's a piece of opera, and in the old operas you get a part called cadenza where one instrument plays by itself. Well one of the winning players was "splitting"—doing pauses in the middle of words. We had the original score and could see what the words were. Our pauses came at the ends of words, so that fitted in with the original. But the adjudicators were old bandsmen who'd never heard the original, and they wouldn't agree with our interpretation.'

The music changes. The traditional communication shifts into competitive display. It becomes not music for an audience, but music for an adjudicator. This is seen in the music specially composed for brass bands: music by contestmen for contestmen. It is music that can be *marked*. In operatic and older march music it was often possible for a band with four good soloists to win their contests, since most of the other instrumentalists only had minor parts. The new music is composed so as to 'go round the band' giving each individual some work to do, bringing his strengths and weaknesses to the adjudicator's attention. Such music immediately raises technical standards, and makes long hours of band practice like the one at the opening of this chapter, quite essential.

'Nowadays, we're a lot more fanatical really. These big bands, it sounds funny to say it, like the Lindley Band that won the Belle Vue Championship in 1900—well they wouldn't have been able to *play* some of the stuff that our local band plays now.'

Contestmen have raised technical standards, but they have lost the bands much of their old audience. More and more, players play to players.

'The stuff we play now, it's difficult. More difficult, and people like me, we like it. I know what to listen for. I liked that last Test Piece at Belle Vue. I knew what there was in it, and waited for it to come out. You had to *listen* for it coming out. But other people don't like it much. I don't *enjoy* it as much as the old pieces.'

Contestmen have also altered the ethics of the movement. Whereas the idealists thought, and still do, in terms of loyalty to the band—the contestmen think primarily of winning. And one good way of winning is to poach good players from other bands—or to join a winning band yourself.

'Borrowing' players for contest day is common, and contest regulations often recognise that it can't be stopped. Generally they try to limit it—perhaps allowing a band to 'borrow' four players. So one good player begins to appear for several bands. Conductors have to curb their impatience ('Tom, he was a good conductor, but a bit erratic. Sometimes he threw his baton at them') or their band is 'borrowed' bit by bit and never returns. Borrowing quickly turns into poaching.

'Afterwards we had a few pints, and they got talking: "When you gonna come and join us?" And they say: "Come on, you want to come up here", and there's an attraction with a band that's winning prizes. They say: "You can have any position you want, you can play any position." A lot of it's pub talk, but that's the way they are. If we had all the good players we've trained up, and who've left for other bands, we should be in the first section now.'

The morality of competition extends into the contests. For even if you've borrowed or poached players, you will still have some instrumentalists weaker than others. In test pieces which 'go round' the band, the temptation is to let your best players 'double up' and play your weaker contestants' parts as well as their own.

'It's not legal, but what can you do about it? You can't tell who's playing unless you have a man standing behind each player. The only thing that stops it much is the ridicule you get, if you're left out. People will laugh at you, and say "Ooh! Look at you!" '

But besides altering and restricting the movement in these ways, poaching cuts back growth. It substitutes theft for training. Bands are less and less likely to take trouble over training young players, if stronger bands wait for the moment to pounce. The situation is like that of Rugby League—which is also strongly rooted, yet incapable of growth, partly because the strong clubs prey on the weak.

At the same time as the contestmen have built an ethic which damages recruitment, the bands also feel frustrated by the local authorities and their schools. For the best recruiting ground of all would be the schools—if only their musical training could become less orchestral, and more brass band centred. But in this sense, local schools are not 'local' at all. Their policies and goals derive from the mobile middle class to whom the brass band world is largely unknown. Huddersfield schools are very musical. They have five school-children's orchestras, but no bridge with the brass bands of their fathers. Most bandsmen tell stories of young boys whose school disapproved of their attending band practice, and usually the school wins. Consequently the main lines of recruitment are now almost entirely through the family. The young cornet players who are common on the brass band scene almost always have fathers in the movement.

Championship Final

All contests lead to the Championship Final at Belle Vue. This Belle Vue Final began at 10.30 a.m. All the nearby pubs had coaches drawn up outside, whilst the bands within, liquorless in full uniform, polished up their test piece.

The final was held in the 'All-in Wrestling' Stadium. Around it the switchback rumbled, fairground staff bawled over megaphones, pop music came fuzzily out of the roundabouts. The bandsmen disliked it:

'They should stop it for a day. It's a bit undignified, I think.'

The Stadium holds 8,000 and by 10.30 a.m. there were already three or four thousand people there. The adjudicators were high up in a box on the right. They remained in this box, locked and hidden, throughout the contest. It was on the side nearest to the Roller Coaster, the fun fair and the side shows.

Twenty-two bands had qualified for the final, and each was due to play the eleven-minute test piece. The audience therefore were going to hear the same piece of music, specially commissioned for its 'testability', twenty-two times. The bands drew for order. It is recognised that it is a disadvantage to be drawn early. As the draw becomes known, the crowd alters. There were always three or four thousand in the Stadium, but some supporters come in for particular bands, and then drift out again. When the great works bands appear, such as Black Dyke Mills, the audience rises to seven or eight thousand.

The listeners were almost entirely working class. A few old men wore flat caps and mufflers. Most were dressed as for an outing. Odd people, here and there, defined its character—gnarled hands, a general set of the head, people eating sandwiches as they listened intently, talking in normal conversational tones. Silence was not demanded. A band came on the platform, its conductor waited for the quietest moment he could, and then they began. The audience discussed the conductor, criticised soloists, argued about correct intonation, suggested marks. Throughout the day there was a perpetual activity of assessment—a general thinking out aloud. The audience was three-quarters male, and most were forty or over. The young people there were usually part of family groups. Young performers were always pointed out as evidence of the movement's virility.

The test piece was called 'Island Heritage'. Its three sections were titled 'Westward Ho!', 'Strange Encounter' and 'The White Cliffs of Dover'. The writer of the contest programme had supplied the audience with a story for the music. The composer had refused to write one. In the programme 'story' the first movement began with 'A great full-rigged ship setting out on a journey of adventure', the second movement was a story of 'Redskin Braves', and the third 'a great ship in full sail, the west wind now astern'.

There were a large variety of interpretations, and each of the twenty-two performances was argued out aloud as 'very musical' or 'bit pedestrian' or 'too much of a sameness'.

In a poorer performance, part of the audience disappeared behind newspapers. You could tell the common assessment by watching the newspapers come up or go down. To the untrained ear, the best half-dozen bands played the piece faultlessly. It was a popular test piece with the audience, who were accustomed to the day-long repetition.

> 'At home we only have one record—a brass band piece—but we haven't got a gramophone player. We have this record and we keep taking it round to our friends, and getting them to play it. We think it's marvellous, but whenever they put it on, they're not really keen.'

Each in their turn the bands entered the wrestling ring and sat down on wooden chairs. All wore different uniforms. Quite common was red and gold, some had green, others blue. One band—from Grimethorpe Colliery—wore evening dress. All the conductors had lounge suits. As the day went on, uniformed players who had finished mingled with the audience. It became harder and harder to remember how bands had performed the piece five hours before. At four o'clock the last band came on. People were announcing who they thought had won places one to six. Support grew for Black Dyke Mills as the winner of the Championship Shield and Cup. None of the Huddersfield bands were backed as winner—it had been a day for the works bands, not those supported by public subscription.

The last band finished 'Island Heritage' at 4.15 p.m. The stadium was packed. The box was unlocked, the three adjudicators came out and were met with great applause. Three silver-haired men, each was introduced to the audience. One was referred to as 'The Uncrowned King of Scotland'. They settled on the platform like high priests of the movement, whilst a man in evening dress did the announcements. He now read out aloud a rather brief acknowledgement, from the Queen, of the Band's Loyal Address, and said how honoured everyone present was. Then followed presentations of certificates to three bandsmen who had each given fifty years' service to the movement. Next, presentations of medals to outstanding bandsmen: the one who got the gold was near to tears. Finally, the results.

Number six was announced first. It was Black Dyke Mills. There was stunned silence, then cries of anger, disagreement, astonishment. Booing began, then died away as number five was declared. As the compère read through the first five places, indignation mounted: only one band was approved. Finally, the winner— Fairey Aviation. Applause was very restrained. People gathered their flasks and sandwich papers and walked out. Arguments broke out, claims were made that the cornet player had blown wrong notes.

The Fairey Band climbed back into the ring. It was announced that they would play an item of their own choice. Perhaps a little shaken by their victory the cornet players took a few moments to get their lips set again. Much to the audience's pleasure the cornet player actually played a string of wrong notes. This set everyone in a happier mood, and Fairey played the theme tune from Dvorak's 'New World Symphony'. It seemed calculated to show the weaknesses of a brass band playing borrowed music. Tempi were ironed out, speeded up or slowed down. The mood switched arbitrarily. It was played with no reference to orchestral performance. Finally, the National Anthem, joyously decorated with long, high fanfares. 'A credit to the movement' said one man.

Conclusion

Brass bands are one of the very many organisations whose coherence, through local ties, common encapsulation by 'them', or the mole-like energy of the linkmen, embodies the astonishingly varied structure of working-class activity. They share many qualities with the Rugby League clubs and their supporters (consider the annual, costly pilgrimage that both make to Wembley in the hope of converting London). And in some ways (like their excessive interest in technicality) they remind you of the jazz clubs, those other minority musicians whose room their committee shares. But above all they have to be measured against the working men's club. Those too had their idealist beginnings. The clubs, like the bands, were associated with the temperance movement, and teetotallers still occupy positions of power in them. But beer has proved best. It has created a social group, capable of considerable diversification, whereas the bands' very limited centre is the skill of contestmen and linkmen.

Their relationship with local life can be misunderstood. Brass bands play for charity in the parks, play on church processions, play before the Rugby League match, or on Whit walks and old folks' outings. They belong to the rhetoric of working-class life. In a time of extreme crisis, such as the Great Strike, they might emerge for a moment as a voice of protest and unity. They are one of the reserves of community. But in the normal tenor of life they are not so central to community as they may seem. They were originally cut off by their failure to come to terms with the clubmen. They are rooted in locality chiefly through kinship entry and the network of linkmen. Only the clubmen could add density to this. But more strikingly the rise of contestmen has led them into a tight minority position. They now spend much of their time playing a highly sophisticated 'non-music'. It is a 'non-music' calling for a high degree of expertise and devotion to a fairly narrow set of technical skills. It is exclusive—only mastered after long practice. And it is markable. It is oddly like the complex 'non-English' and 'non-mathematics' that secondary school teachers have evolved because of examination pressures.

It is interesting that this substantial pocket of music is so untouched by the mass media—much more so even than the resilient singing style of the clubs. The advertising poster of the boozy trombonist similarly bespeaks the unseen wall surrounding much working-class life. This is no loss. But when the wall stands between the orchestral interests of the schools and the brass music of the parents, an opportunity has been missed. Part of the school's function is to provide an exit from the restrictions of the locality; and what the schools can open up is part of the central culture of the race. One imagines that a musical genius—Bach, a Bartok or Britten—could use both the inheritance of high music and this sub-culture of the brass bands in a way that would be the ultimate criticism of both bandroom and school. As it is, there is waste. And yet, there's an extraordinary strength there. Just as the teetotal president of the working men's club can drink his Lucozade among the high singing and pints of a Saturday night, and be quite at home, so with the idealists among the contests of Belle Vue. The contest satisfies the idealist too, but for him as a kind of spiritual struggle, a musical methodism: '*to make better music, to make music better*'. The mixture of sportsman, clubman and the strains of 'Jerusalem' gives you the very texture of the working man's life in Huddersfield: even the strikeless, school-dominated, affluent Huddersfield of today.

Chapter Four

AT THE CLUB

The Working Men's Club and Institute Union was founded in London in 1862. It received support from the Prince of Wales, eleven Dukes, the Earls of Shrewsbury and Lichfield. It was backed by bankers like Lord Rothschild, and industrialists like Sir Thomas Brassey. Brassey presented the Union with 500 copies of his book *Work and Wages*. 'Certain it is that so comprehensive a list of distinguished men and women of the Victorian era, led by Lord Chancellors and Archbishops, was never before or since attached to any scheme.'[1] The organising spirit was Henry Solly, a Unitarian minister and famous spokesman of the temperance movement.[2] The Union's first President was Lord Brougham. Brougham had worked hard to establish the Mechanics Institutes, a generation earlier. Basically the institutes—of which the Huddersfield Mechanics' Institute was one of the most notable— were evening institutes, financed by the middle-class industrialists, at which the working class were taught both useful technical skills and such inner mysteries of *laissez faire* economics as 'the iron law of wages' by which it was hoped they would fulfil the duties proper to their station of life more efficiently and less restlessly.[3] The Mechanics' Institutes had failed, but in old age Lord Brougham was spirited enough to join in the new wave of missionary work to settle the working class. The YMCA, the Boys' Brigade, the Boys' Club movement—and later, even the Primrose League—were all penetrating the working class.[4] Solly

[1] *Our Fifty Years* by B. T. Hall (1912).
[2] Solly's own account is to be found in his *Working Men's Clubs and Educational Institutes* (Whitefield, 1867).
[3] Tylecote, M. *The Mechanics Institutes of Yorkshire and Lancashire*.
[4] Sir George Williams, the YMCA's founder, put it simply 'great power is being given to the working classes. How is it to be turned to the best

and Brougham saw the working men's clubs as a superior approach to the Mechanics' Institutes, because the clubs would emphasise recreation, and in that atmosphere advance 'Education and Temperance'. It was an attack on the 'intemperance, ignorance, improvidence and religious indifference' of the working class, and aimed quite sharply to take working men out of the pub and into a club 'free from intoxicating drinks'. The clubs were an answer to the cry 'What are we to do with our reformed drunkards?'

For twenty years the workmen tolerated it. Lord Brougham was followed as President by Lord Rosebery, and then Dean Stanley of Westminster. 'Lady Augusta Stanley and the Dean frequently invited large parties to Westminster Abbey and to tea at the Deanery.' Then, seeing no reason why the normal process of democratic election, which prevailed in the individual clubs shouldn't apply to the central council too, they pushed the proposal at the annual meeting. They even proposed Bradlaugh as a Vice-President. The Dukes and Earls all left. There were no more teas at the Deanery. The working class took over the movement.

It only remained for them to bring their beer in, and—despite the assumptions of the industrialists, aristocracy, clerics, and liberal reformers—there was the germ for a movement which has given its shape to working-class community. Said the first working-class President, 'Each club should be altogether free from all vexatious infantile restrictions on the consumption of intoxicating drinks and all similar matters.'

Huddersfield today has seventy clubs affiliated to the national Working Men's Club and Institute Union. With Denis Marsden and Sheila Jackson, I visited sixteen of these and interviewed 100 members. The following account is based on this.

Most of the local communities in Huddersfield have their working men's club. Most commonly the club owns some blackened stone-built house which they have converted, over the years, to their own uses. Frequently it is a large Edwardian home

---

account? Is Bradlaugh to be allowed to have his say. . . .?'—from *Life of Sir George Williams* by J. E. Hodder Williams (Hodder and Stoughton, 1906) as quoted in *Education and the Labour Movement 1870-1920* by Brian Simon (Lawrence & Wishart, 1965).

which the club took over soon after the Great War. Moldgreen
Working Men's Club moved out of their original wooden hut in
1925 and bought themselves, with the aid of a brewery loan, the
house of the local doctor. It is severe and gloomy, and surrounded
by a small and utterly neglected garden. Yet it is completely built
into the community, and not the least of its attractions is the
sound of children playing in the schoolyard beyond.

Some of the clubs do not achieve this scale. Forest Hill Working
Men's Club is merely one house amongst many others in an
isolated line of back-to-back houses high on one of the ridges
running into the town. It has only fifty members, almost all
coming from this same street. When we first arrived the club was
closed—it opens only in the evenings; but there was no difficulty
in discovering the President, squatting on his doorstep some few
yards away. The club is hemmed in on every side by difficult,
unbuildable ground, and clusters of small bungalows taking
advantage of the height and view. How the street comes to be
there at all on that steep and awkward hillside is difficult to
conceive. It looks like some stray building speculation of seventy
years ago. But isolation has made for intimacy of living. It has
had its club since the last century. There is no sign to distinguish
it; merely a crateful of empty lemonade bottles on the doorstep
where the milk would usually stand.

Other clubs, with more space, have room for a bowling green.
And whereas the surrounding garden may be tangled and weed-
grown, the 'green' is cherished with extraordinary care. Large
sums of money are willingly spent on hiring experts to improve its
condition; though at one the club steward took three years to
repair the damage the last 'expert' had done.

Inside the clubs all have, of course, their bar. They usually have
too a large general lounge, and perhaps a smaller women's room.
It is a precise reversal of the public house layout. There may be a
games and billiards room, and perhaps upstairs a place for the
club concerts.

Many of the clubs had recently been re-decorated in quite
contemporary fashion, and many others were hesitating over such
a move, or resisting it and being very conscious of resisting it.
This sometimes turned out to be entangled with their strategy
of remaining intact, a male society.

In the very centre of Huddersfield stands the largest club of all, the Friendly and Trades Club. Seventy-two Unions and 300 Friendly Societies are affiliated to it. It is the central Working Men's Club, the meeting place of the Friendly Societies, and the focus for local Trade Unions—whose members are automatically members of the club too. The building was formerly the old Mechanics' Institute and the letters are to be seen boldly incised along the full length of the building. A small back lane, Friendly Street, runs alongside it. Immediately opposite is the equally blackened and rather older Huddersfield Primitive Methodist Chapel, where the continuation of Friendly Street changes its name to Primitive Street. A quiet last-century tableau.

Origins

The origins of the clubs were difficult to trace. Sometimes the foundation date was chiselled above the door, and faithfully recorded beneath the club's name in the annual report. It was therefore well known to the members, but it was useless to seek for any ulterior authority for this claim. Records were seldom kept, and little attention paid to the history of the club. This largely held true for the clubs that were founded in the last quarter of the nineteenth century as many of them were. In clubs which were founded in the first twenty years of this century we could often be directed to the oldest member. Only once we heard of some of the old minute books which had, accidentally, been preserved—but no one could find them.

> 'Some of them old minute books make very interesting reading— very amusing. Ah were looking at one that said about club alterations —it were right, like: they knew what they wanted, but the way it were spelt! Well, some of them fellers left school when they were eight or nine.'

It was generally so. Working men's clubs had emerged indistinctly out of the flurry of working-class co-operative activity between 1875 and 1914. We discovered one stray founded in 1935, and one started on a new housing estate in 1964. Sometimes they were offshoots of an original Trade Union club, and still retained close connections with the unions. At the Dyers and

Finishers Working Men's Club, the Club Secretary and Trade Union Secretary are the same man. 'Two jobs for one wage,' said a member. 'It used to be in an old barn over yonder across Wellington Street. They all called it "t'old Cobden" till t'bobbies shifted us.'

But the only effective touch of history in Huddersfield is the fact that you can't get a drink at the Friendly on Sundays. 'We don't open on Sundays—it's a relic of the old union days. They were strong Methodists—six days shalt thou labour and all that.'

Few traces of such a past were left. Whatever the origins of any particular club, the local community had shaped it to their own active ends. The members cared very little about the club's old history. The club didn't exist for them in that sense, as an old-established school or college exists historically for *its* members. To them the club meant the people whom they knew to talk to, or had known before they died. It was all intensely personal, and minute books and records were seen as the rather trivial fringe to club activity which the law required should be preserved for a brief space of time, and no longer.

How They Join

A new member must be proposed and seconded by two members of the club. His name is then put up on the board in the club for two weeks so that any club member who objects can raise his objections at the next club committee meeting. . . .

'They'll say, "Oh, he's a trouble maker; we're not having him." '

If the man is not opposed, he is allowed to join for 4/-, and on payment of another 2/- he obtains all the benefits of affiliation of the Club and Institute Union—for example, access to any affiliated club, and to the convalescent homes.

Members are allowed to bring in friends as guests, but, by law they must pay for everything which their guest has in the club, and when the guest is signed in he receives a paper slip.

Caution

Visitors are strictly prohibited from obtaining or attempting to obtain, by payment, directly or indirectly, any excisable articles while visiting the Club.

Should any visitor be detected in doing so, he will be immediately removed from the premises, and the Member who introduced him will be expelled, on the fact being proved.

Like many other of the formalities, these are merely designed to placate 'them', and their agents the police. We seldom saw these rules observed.

Members whom we picked at random in the clubs usually had relatives in the same club. At the weekend, they had brothers, sons, fathers or uncles, mothers, wives, daughters or fiancées with them. Everybody we asked had neighbours in the club, some said 'dozens'; one estimated that half the people in the long road where he lived belonged to the club. And these ties shaded off into school friends and work mates. Less firm ties merged easily into the general code of friendliness, so that the edges of groups blurred.

Anybody who gets inside the clubs must have a very substantial community of interest and attitude with the members. Once inside, the whole tendency is towards conservation of the more stable elements in local society. And this is not because club members are old as a group, though older members tend to have more influence where tradition and lore are oral.

The fact that the clubs can flourish, whilst imposing 'old-fashioned' patterns of behaviour on their members, argues that they draw upon a large and stable community. People who are deliberately barred from the clubs are usually labelled 'rowdy' elements . . . 'none of them strangers and West Indians causing bother.'

There are very few business men or small tradesmen in the clubs, but what few there are prefer to merge quietly into the club's ranks, and take no part in the various committees. 'They've got their own clubs and political clubs. It's all working men here.'

From this angle pubs are 'society', where you might mix with strangers, must dress more smartly, remember your manners a bit more. But the club has the atmosphere of home.

'Ah never go into a pub at all now. Clubs are much more sociable like. Look at this. Ah couldn't rest me legs across a chair in t'pub. Here it's like being at home. As long as Ah don't put me feet on t'seat, Ah'm all right.'

44

At the Club

Daily Scene

One way in which a club differs from a public house is that it can decide during which hours it shall sell beer. Only on Sundays must its hours coincide with those of the local pubs. The club is still open and used of course even when the bar shutters are down. This allows the club hours to be moulded to the needs of members, and to the local cycle of work and leisure. Very many of the men at Oakes Working Men's Club work in the local woollen mill; the Trafalgar Working Men's Club members are largely employed in the I.C.I. works across the road. Obviously they want their club open during the lunch breaks. More than that; hours are chosen to suit the members' 'natural breaks', and not the needs of 'them'. One club planned its hours with special care because 'There's always people dodging out from work!'

Working needs not only dictate lunchtime opening. Some clubs re-open their bars as early as 4 p.m. for early evening shift workers to enjoy a quiet drink, along with a read of the papers. During the lunch hours the clubs are seldom full. The old men may be there, and perhaps someone is off work through illness. There may be a handful of local workers and perhaps a soldier or sailor home on leave. Very little drinking is done; mostly it is talking, reading the paper, playing cribbage.

A club may be dominated at lunchtime by a group of pensioners, meeting there as they do every day. But on Saturdays it is different. Many men will be off work and the place will be quite crowded, and on Sundays at this time it will be packed. Regular members attend their own club for a drink before Sunday dinner, even members who have now moved some distance away. Women are not usually allowed in the club at this time, and a gathering is created—kin, workmates, old schoolmates, neighbours— different from that on any other occasion. It cannot be like this in a pub, and in the evenings they may have their wives with them or be visiting other places, or they may have more visitors in their own club. But Sunday lunchtime is a cherished occasion. It doesn't last long. But while it does the notice may go up above the beer pumps 'No ladies will be served at this bar'. Men gamble, make wagers, drink, talk. It's common to see a small girl sitting by her father, who called in from his Sunday morning walk.

Tuesday and Wednesday evenings are quiet ones. Pay day is a long way behind. And Wednesday, end of the financial week, is called 'common sense night'. Thursday night is much busier as some trades get paid then, and Friday and Monday lead in and out of the very busy weekends. At Almondbury, a very flourishing club, we were told: 'Tuesday's our slackest night—there's about forty people in the club.'

At Turnbridge Working Men's Club on a Wednesday evening, there were two or three youths playing billiards, fifteen to twenty men and then as the evening wore on a dozen or so wives and mothers came in. The women gradually took over the seats near the bar. At first the men played dominoes from these seats, and there was only one woman in the club—an old lady, in Irish shawl and slippers coming in to have her jug filled with draught ale. She came in and out three times during the evening, standing at the bar for five minutes and sipping a bottle of beer herself. Once she was passed by a small boy on the same errand. At the end of the evening the men had moved to the far side of the room, away from the women, to gamble at cards. Down at the back a man was washing himself after work.

Washing facilities matter a great deal in some clubs and attract people in, for just that purpose, on a Thursday or Friday evening. In any club a workman can have a dowse down, of course, in a way he never could in a public house. Some clubs go further. At Oakes the notice said: 'Baths available Thursday onwards' and about a dozen members took advantage each week. At Lindley Working Men's Club there are four baths. These are used on a Thursday and Friday night. Thursday night is for women only— which means members' closest feminine relatives, wives, mothers, daughters, sisters. There is a charge of fourpence.

At the weekends, the clubs are at their liveliest. But it is holiday spirit rather than holiday clothes. The lounge of the Friendly and Trades Club on a Saturday evening is much noisier than the lounge of a pub would normally be. Some of the men and women are dressed up for Saturday night, but most are in their daily clothes and had taken no special trouble before coming out. One or two in flat caps, but not best flat caps; one man with a flower in his buttonhole; and upstairs three hundred people in the Concert Room.

Saturday night is Concert Night and Sunday night is Bingo Night, though one or two clubs disapprove of either one or the other, or both. Bingo accounts largely for the flourishing financial state of the clubs. They have never been richer. But drinking, and concerts, and gambling, each deserve treatment of their own.

Drinking

'Drunken men have been seen through the windows of one of these clubs, lying on wooden forms. . . .' (Rowntree 1902)

'. . . the friendly mug of beer—primordial cell of British social life —supplies the social bond. . . .' (Booth 1889)

Working men's clubs are a co-operative venture in the purchase and sale of beer and spirits. Each offers a choice of several draught beers, and the brews are changed ruthlessly as members demand. A public house is almost always 'tied' to a brewery, and only sells that brewery's draught beer. With bottled beer there is, customarily, a slightly wider choice. Very few public houses are privately owned 'free houses' selling what beer they choose. In the centre of Huddersfield there is only one 'free house'.

At Oakes Working Men's Club: 'You go across the road and have a pint at the pub there, and then come and try it here. We're all shareholders here, y'know, all shareholders.' Consequently the breweries are very anxious for their goodwill. They often offer large loans at nominal interest for club extensions and decorations. The club members seldom permit this to dictate their choice of beer, and this can be embarrassing for their President. At one club a £1,700 loan from the brewery had never been paid off at all in forty-one years, the club merely paying the 1% interest. 'We'll never get anywhere till we pay off that loan. Every year I have to go cap in hand to the brewery, and the Directors say "How is it you've spent such and such . . . and why don't you sell our beer?"'

Members claim great powers of discrimination with the beers, and immediately stop orders for any beer that falls below expected standards.

'Norton Ales? That's powerful stuff! Fred Hargreaves drank that.

47

He's not *dead*—but it finished *his* betting, y'know. Club sent him to Grange-over-Sands to t'Convalescent Home. Ah tell you what; that Norton Ale would kill *elephants*, never mind men!'

Freedom of purchase, backed by a discriminating and demanding membership, has put the club in an interesting position. There is an excellent draught beer brewed which is sold in surrounding Yorkshire. But it cannot be obtained in Huddersfield public houses because the pubs are in the possession of rival concerns. The beer, though good, is blocked out of town. Except for the clubs. In almost every one a pint of this ale could be bought. The beer was chosen and sold on its merits, quite regardless of the major brewery strategy which limits the range of the pub drinker.

Draught beer costs as much as it does in the cheapest room of a pub. But the members know that profits are turned over to them in various forms. Spirits are very much cheaper, though they are not so often drunk, except by the women. This is very useful at Christmas when working men make their annual purchase of whisky, rum, port and sherry. The club fills its cellars just to give them this discount.

Did all this situation make for heavy drinking and drunkenness? Obviously since a club might be open for another hour after the neighbouring pubs had closed, there were fine opportunities for heavy drinkers to move on, and continue. This happens, particularly during the annual holidays, but not very much. There were real forces making against this use of their facilities. Heavy drinking and rowdiness were exceptionally rare. They happened of course:

'It finished up just like a ranch-house, just like the films. I stood there and screamed. They were all swinging chairs at each other. When I got to the door, somebody said: "Good-night, love, come again." '

There was plenty of drunkenness in the surrounding pubs. How was it that drinking seldom went far in the clubs?

Obviously a member who was habitually unpleasant when he had had too much to drink could be expelled. But this only explained the extreme case. We asked members the difference between drinking in a pub and drinking in a club: 'I always feel

that when you are in a pub, and your glass gets down, they all
start looking at you.'

There was no pressure to buy. You could sit in a club all night
and never buy a drink, and nobody cared.

> 'Y'not compelled to have a drink. You can come in and read the
> paper or have a game of dominoes and nobody pesters you. Some
> of the old people can't afford a drink anyway. People come in
> Tuesday, Wednesday and Thursday and stop in all evening and never
> touch a drop. Only at week-ends they'd have a drink. Y'can sit with
> a gill in y'hand all night in a club; y'couldn't do it in a pub. But we've
> a few teetotallers here, you know.'

It was true. At Rawthorpe Working Men's Club the treasure-
was a teetotaller like his father. At Lindley the secretary was teer
total, and at another club one official was so keen a teetotaller
that he attended international teetotallers' conferences on the
continent. The teetotallers, though few, seemed at ease and un-
embarrassed in the club atmosphere. Obviously though the clubs
were, at one level, a co-operative society dealing chiefly in
draught beer, they had other appeals to their members.

The breweries' thrusting advertising campaigns had intruded
very little into this world. The clubs were not compelled to take
posters if they didn't want them, and were very free from the
advertising nick-nacks—all those wall plaques or illuminated
name plates—common in the surrounding pubs. Once, it is true,
we noticed a particularly assertive poster for Otley Ales, and
inquired how many pumps they had drawing that brew. It was a
joke. The club didn't sell the beer, and never had. They took the
poster as a consolation to the ever-unsuccessful Otley traveller.
And once we heard that Yarnold's Ales had made a bid, but:

> 'No; they don't like Yarnold's beer here. T'brewery has tried to
> introduce it. Ah remember traveller bringing a barrel. It were free
> while he was here, he paid for t'lot. They supped it then, y'know.
> They did that! They supped it like *bloody wolves*! But when he were
> gone nobody would touch it. It's like lead in y'belly is that stuff.
> When Ah had some, Ah felt as if Ah'd swallowed yon plumb-line
> hanging from t'window there.'

There was quiet gambling, for small sums of money, going at
most times. Most of the gambling took place during the period

when women were not allowed into the club. If women were present the gambling would be at the furthest physical distance from them—the players moving away, as women occupied more and more seats. A woman shouldn't know too much about a man's money.

Gambling was never for large sums, nor did it ever seem very intense. Except perhaps for some women playing Bingo. No one regarded Bingo as gambling; and Bingo accounted for all the new buildings. Most clubs had a Bingo night for their building fund. It was especially popular on Sunday evening when the bye-law made by 'them' stamped out much rival entertainment. In the pub it was even forbidden to sing on Sundays. In the club you could raise the rafters if that was the general mood.

A club being a more or less secluded place into which the police do not easily get entry, it is an obvious situation for passing on betting slips to a bookmaker. Professional book-makers were usually members of the clubs. One club had two bookmakers and a certain element of competition. But it was not the bookmaker who usually took the bets. He employed his 'runner' to do this, bring them to his office, and distribute the winnings.

> 'Every club has its own bookie's runner. Saturday dinner-time on that table over there, you get Aga Khan, de Rochefort and t'lot. It pays good money y'see. It averages 1/6d. in the pound in these parts. Like down town there'll be a runner for six or seven firms. Well he might collect £50—that's fifty one and sixpences for himself.'

Sometimes the runner might be a pensioner supplementing his income, or a disabled worker—but the commission was high enough for it to attract able bodied men.

A policeman is in a difficult position as a club member. Relations with the police matter a lot, and were frequently introduced into conversation.

> 'Ah went up and met Inspector Bradley—he said "Ah'm very pleased to meet you". Ah said, "Aye, but Ah'm none so pleased to see you." '

A policeman usually comes from a working-class background, but it is police policy to push up the educational requirements in such a way as to recruit primarily from the ex-grammar school boys. On joining the force the working-class boy has to readjust his private relationships all round. On duty and off duty he is still a policeman. And since the working class may indulge in a host of minor, illegal activities he may find friends hard to come by. This is of course well known, and the official reaction is to house all policemen in groups together, encourage police clubs and wives' clubs and so inbreed their social life. Nevertheless a policeman can still join a working men's club, and at Newsom they were rather proud that: 'We've got police as members—we've *let* 'em join.'

Certainly it called for uncommon tact—at one we visited they had had a popular police member who had brought to a fine perfection the art of sensing the beginning of some illegal activity, and moving into the next room. At another it was a case of a more down-to-earth give and take:

> 'They come round to the back here to have a smoke, and one of them said, "For heaven's sake, if you're going to drink after hours, pull the curtains."'

The typical position is that which we saw one night. There was the usual 'No Gambling . . . by order of the Committee' notice. The bookie's runner was sitting next to the president. He kept glancing at the door, and as newcomers arrived, got up and walked over to them. He slipped a piece of paper into the member's hand with a certain crude caution, quietly exchanged a little racing gossip, and returned to his drink with the president.

Crime

There is no crime in the clubs. At least none that members would acknowledge as that. A man who burgled a house, stole from a post office, helped set up a bank raid, would get no supporting solidarity here. Members would be just as shocked as the Methodist congregations in the same roads.

But stolen goods are bought and sold all the time. Most working-class families, I think, have handled small amounts of stolen property all their lives. It may be no more than bundles of firewood from a works, a spanner and hammer from the

factory, bricks or planks from a builder. In the clubs you can buy
a little more, not much. You can get a roll of cloth from the mills
('they'd only throw it away, it's a short cut'). You can buy
vegetables, eggs or chickens—which may come from a man's
own allotment, but just as likely come from the back door of the
city market or a works canteen. No attention is drawn to all
this, but none of it is concealed either. It is not thought to be
wrong, but everyone knows that it's best not to say exactly where
a suit length or a Christmas bird came from, since magistrates
subscribe to a different code of right and wrong—especially with
regard to property.

It isn't very easy to define right and wrong in the clubs, but
it's a very strict difference for all that. It is always wrong to steal
money. Violence is always wrong. Theft from workmates or
landladies is vicious. Theft from corner shops is utterly wrong.
Breaking into the gas meter isn't so much wrong as stupid. But
'nicking a bit' from Woolworth's is all right. So is stealing small,
useful articles from all large employers. A certain amount of face-
to-face cheating is no great matter for shame either, even within
the working-class community. The coalman who delivers five
sacks instead of six, the milkman who charges for an undelivered
pint each week, are using their wits rather than breaking the code.
Similarly the perpetual pastime of avoiding paying your fare
on the bus (by burying yourself in the evening paper, or staring
out of the window, or falling deep into conversation) only saves
a few pennies. You do that just to keep in trim, to add another
little incident to the day. If a strict middle class property code
were to be applied in the clubs, most of the members would
eventually end up in court. Nevertheless they are probably more
free from crime than the London clubs subscribed to by bishops,
members of parliament, and leaders of industry.

Concert

Huddersfield cannot support a variety theatre. But of the sixteen
clubs we visited, only two had no concerts at all. The city is
on the fringe of the rich concert area centred on Barnsley and
the mining districts—but there is nothing here on the scale that
takes place in South Yorkshire—where a club has been known

to fly a star over from America, or pay more than the London Palladium. In the mining area around Barnsley and in the great stretch of working men's clubs from Tyneside to Durham, the clubs are dominated by the pits.

'Ah were in a club in Barnsley at ten to two one day, and Ah thought the barman had gone mad. He started drawing pints and he went on until he had over a hundred standing on the bar. Then the miners came in. Straight back it went—to wash the coal dust out of their throats. Only four of them stayed.'

Larger thirsts means larger clubs, with more benefits for sick or healthy miners. Many of the coalfield clubs build bungalows for retired miners and rent them out at 7/6d a week. And areas like those put on lavish concerts, to which Huddersfield people sometimes go on a special club trip:

'They employ men all night simply to pick up the empty bottles and carry them away in baskets. It has gardens and greenhouses and all. They employ three full-time gardeners there—not one, three! It were a real friendly club. You could feel it as soon as you went through t'door. It looks nowt outside, but when you get in there's lights and decorations—it's lovely, fair lovely inside.'

Huddersfield is much quieter. At the first concert we went to, the secretary said: 'A tenor or a soprano, or a bass—straight singers—that's all out now, they've got to mix it.'

The singer for the evening agreed with this. He was a man of fifty or so and had been in the business for twenty years. 'There's been a change in the last ten years. These young 'uns, they won't come to listen to "The Road to Mandalay" every week. They want something out of "Top Ten". It's different at every club. At Barnsley they like a singer more.'

This did not prevent him from starting with an impassioned old love song, 'Marta, Rambling Rose of the Wild Wood'. He followed with 'The Wayward Wind', then a cowboy song, with which he was not quite so happy, although he did his best to look 'mean', and jogged up and down keeping time. Like the pianist, his style was such that a piece, while it could never be called modern, could not be dated. The concert secretary chaired the meeting, taking his responsibilities seriously. He rang an electric bell and said 'Order please' and when the noise failed to subside completely, he said more sternly, 'Can we have complete order all round the room, *please*,' and got complete silence. There was not much enthusiasm for the singing; one or two older people half closed their eyes during 'Marta', their lips moving to the words. The pianist's playing of 'Lollipop' was very well received by the younger women in the audience, who sang in support.

Probably the only person who thoroughly enjoyed all parts of the concert was the steward's little daughter, aged eight or so, who sat on the bar at the back of the room and joined in the newer songs. The pianist had started with a slow piece, and the secretary grumbled: 'Not like an old-timer. They used to start with a march. It was all marches in them days.'

The distinction between the singers with good voices and those who had to 'put a popular song every other one' is clearly shown on the club concert programme. The good singers were described as 'Vocalists', and less good as 'Versatile' and the worst as 'Popular Vocalists'.

If the club can afford it, the ideal concert bill will include a comedian as well as a singer. 'It's difficult getting comedians. They all tell me how expensive it is to buy a new script.'

The comedians were unlucky. A singer could return year after year with substantially the same act. But people had long memories for jokes.

'Nothing falls as flat as a joke they've heard before—it's dead before it's left their mouth, and everyone's turning to each other and saying, "This is how this one finishes".'

Under this pressure, many of the comedians took the easy way out.

'Trouble is now, that most of these comedians have got too filthy and the younger people coming in won't have it.'

The arbiter of taste in the concert is the concert secretary. His job is to fill the programme with acts suited to the members of his particular club. In choosing a turn, apart from the known opinions of the members, the concert secretary goes to auditions which are taking place all the time in different clubs all over Yorkshire.

'Ah get first choice, but it's too expensive now, competing against those bigger clubs from South Yorkshire. We have to have two or three raffles in t'evening now to pay t'artist.'

Mutual Helpfulness

Because they impinge at so many points in the lives of their members, the clubs cannot ignore the disruptions caused by accident, illness, bereavement, retirement. The Victorian phrase 'mutual helpfulness' was written into the original charter of the Club and Institute Union.

The effects of misfortunes come very suddenly in a manual worker's life, and help is organised when it is required, guided by custom and the circumstances of the club and its members. A man from Almondbury said:

'Ah once had twelve weeks off work with yellow jaundice, and they gave me two or three sums like a pound or thirty shillings. It helped out.'

At Lindley they had a young member whose leg was badly mauled in an accident; the club proposed a bowls match as a benefit. The secretary wrote to the Yorkshire Bowling Association for permission to play on a Sunday; another member in the Yorkshire team contacted the captain ('Ah'll play anywhere to help a club member in trouble'), who picked a Yorkshire team to play Lindley. A charge of sixpence was made, with a tea afterwards (done by members' wives), and a concert in the evening. At the end the member, accompanied by his wife and mother, received £50.

It sometimes happens that a member will behave so badly that he must be expelled. In such a crisis, 'mutual helpfulness' faces a test:

'Only the other week, I had the very painful job of expelling a member from the club. I hated to do it but it had to be done. This chap wasn't a very desirable character—anyway the steward caught him one day behind the bar stealing money. He ran after him and this chap gave him the money back, and asked him not to say anything, but somebody else had seen it. We had a committee meeting and expelled him, but we didn't make it a police job because he was a family man. He had a prison record and he'd have got five years.'

They make the best out of a bad job, and frequently display a humanity broader than that sometimes displayed in the local law courts. It is a disregard springing from long experience of judging character, situation and personality, within the range of everyday situations. The life of the club is not based on written rules or abstract situations, but on personality and precedent.

A big feature in club life (and, for that matter, in the pubs with strong local affiliations) is the trip when coach-loads of members, without wives, ride to Blackpool or the races, with all food and some drink provided.

'We write to a club about half-way back, and stop there until they kick us out.' The breweries usually provided beer for any club functions. 'We just write to them and say we're having a trip and they send us a crate or two. It was nine bottles each last time.'

Moldgreen got the best of both worlds by going to Redcar. 'If y'go to Blackpool y'can only do one thing, but if y'go to Redcar you've got a choice. Y'can go racing or y'can go to the seaside. There's a club convalescent home one-and-a-half miles away and a lot of people go to look round that. We had an old member in there and he liked racing, so when we had a trip he came out to see us.

'But of course it's the children that really matter, isn't it?' There had been a children's outing to Belle Vue the previous week. The children were given half-a-crown to spend, and had tea and ice-cream bought. Seventy-three children went. At Bradley and Colne Bridge 'We have a special children's treat committee. Some people will join the club just to do something for the children.' Turnbridge W.M.C. had just been modernised. 'It cost £2,400 did that job, and we asked members to support us and do without a trip for two years till we got paid off. We kept the kiddies' treat up of course, and their concert.'

And in very many ways the clubs move out to link with other local groups. Perhaps they will lend a room for the local football team to change in, or some of the officials may be common to both groups—part of that chain of organisers who criss-cross so many working-class groupings.

At Bradley the president was also secretary of Bradley and Colne Bridge Old Folks' Treat. 'Last year we had the biggest "do" we've ever had. There were over four hundred guests, and they had tea and a concert.' Free of charge, the club provides the local Darby and Joan Club with a meeting place every Thursday. Upstairs, the local Labour Council meetings are held, free of charge. The Bradley Rangers A.F.C. was founded at the club. And the club secretary is also the secretary of the Bradley and Deighton Brass Band, which practises below in the cellar.

Leadership

Who precisely emerged as leaders in the clubs, and in what did their leadership consist? We were curious to know if there was any monopoly of leadership; that is, if the Club officials turned out to be also Union workers, prominent co-op members, organisers behind local sporting activities, old folks' outings, brass band concerts, district carnivals. Or if there were any firm political connections, perhaps nourished in part by some such 'monopoly of leadership'. And we wondered too, about the effect on club life of the developing state education system which might increasingly draw away the most talented members of the working class.

Each club had its president, secretary, treasurer and committee. All these officials were elected annually by the members in open meeting. In addition the club would have a panel of trustees, who might or might not take a direct part in the day-to-day organisation of the club. ('Some folk think y'can only be a trustee if you're a married man.') The committee, once in office, might break up into small sub-committees concerning themselves with specific interests (social entertainments, sports, a building fund). The sub-committees would be in a large degree autonomous, and have their own bank account. From the sub-committees emerged the familiar figure of the concert secretary, the status of whose office was but little below that of the club secretary proper. Newly-elected committee members would move into office at six-monthly periods, ensuring continuity and stability.

The open meeting was held in mid-week ('so as not to interfere with trade'). Attendance varied considerably. There were packed meetings when the club was faced with difficulties (i.e. to raise a loan or not to raise a loan), and plenty to be said: 'They

E

get up on their hind legs and have a crack, y'know.' Other clubs complained of poor attendance (by 'poor' they meant about 40-50 from a membership of, say, 200). Prosperity, and efficient organisation drew no crowds. 'Members look at the balance sheet; "Club's all right" they say, and they don't bother much. . . .' Consequently some clubs were undecided about whether or not they should give out the annual free beer chits on these nights. Several did, others felt this to be wrong.

The secretary and president drew an annual payment of £10 or £15. Committee members received a nominal 1/- a meeting at some clubs, nothing at all at most. Club members subscribed towards a dinner or coach trip for the retiring officers. One or two clubs felt the difficulty of raising a full committee as required by law, and had to accept some merely nominal members. Most experienced no difficulty at all.

The secretary and president were required to attend the club at least three nights a week, and besides their internal leadership these were the men who faced the outside world on the club's behalf—negotiating loans from building societies or breweries, dealing directly with the Club and Institute Union. They were legally responsible if the club was prosecuted. The secretaries of all the Huddersfield clubs met quarterly and were addressed on club topics (e.g. The Law and the Clubs) by a visiting speaker from the central organisation and one from the local branch of the W.E.A. 'They've got letters behind their names some of 'em. It sometimes makes me wish I had a bit more up here' (tapping his temple). 'But there's many a man in an office couldn't do my job.'

The concert secretaries also had a strong organisation of their own, and came together frequently as a body—to talk, to celebrate, to audition 'turns'.

The club secretaries were not easily distinguished from the rest of the members. They varied in age from men in their middle twenties to others past retirement age. But they were not leaders by virtue of their dominative personal traits. They were noticeably without qualities of leadership as these are still often conceived by schoolmasters, industrialists, army officers. They were quiet, and as officials, informal in manner and tone. At the most their presence might be announced by a heightened watchfulness. They had strong disciplinary powers, which they were expected to use

('Y'can't have a club, to my mind, unless everything is strict'),
but to use very quietly.

Club officials did not derive their authority from being leaders
amongst the working men in an assertive, personal way. Their
authority had to do with their office, and the customs and respects
due to it. Their rightness as officers of the club derived from their
instinctive formulation of the members' desires and hostilities in
an efficient form. There was no sign of the stream of leaders
coming to an end. They were not concerned with breaking new
ground, but with preserving and with strengthening. Functional
leadership went along with social equality. Members were in no
way deferential to their officers, as men, though respectful of the
rights of their office. Hence the difficulty of picking out the
secretary in a crowded club room without actually inquiring.

This being so, much of our further curiosity as regards the
possibly disabling effect of the educational system on a characteristic working-class institution lost its edge. It was apparent that
the qualities by which these men expressed the group feelings in
terms of organisation—tact, sympathy, caution—were not such
as would be withdrawn from working-class living by the educational system as we now know it.

Did it work the other way? Did any working-class boys, having
gone through the grammar schools, then return and join this club
community in the evenings? At the Friendly and Trades Club we
found a former working-class boy who was now a lecturer at
Manchester University. At weekends he seemed impelled to withdraw from the University life, and sometimes spent his time with
his uncle at the club: 'You get this strange feeling of being caught
between two worlds.'

But his role was not an active one, and his visits more occasional
than regular. At Rawthorpe Working Men's Club we found
that an ex-grammar school boy was now, at twenty-five, club
treasurer. He seemed uncomfortable in his relationship to his
fellow officials with whom he had strong differences about club
policy and conduct. When we spoke to him he was about to
resign his post over the seemingly slight question of whether the
club should pay a bill for bad decoration. Otherwise there was
little trace of the ex-grammar school boy. Club life seemed unaffected either way by the education system.

Working men's clubs are non-political. This means they do not subscribe to any political party, and that members may call upon the secretary to stop disturbing political argument. But there is such a large measure of agreement in this homogeneous society that difference of this kind does not often arise. Non-political though the clubs proclaim themselves to be, there are, necessarily, natural connections with the Left. Two clubs were established 'bridges' between the clubs and the local union branches. Here union subscriptions could be paid in, and union meetings held. The secretaries of these clubs also held trade union posts, and so lived as full-time officials.

Other clubs felt this was too much like direct political activity and claimed to have none of it: 'Unions—that's politics, that is. We're non-political. We had to stop a man the other week for monopolising the conversation. We don't mind a bit of it amongst ourselves, but when they monopolise everybody it's different. Same with religion.'

Nevertheless connections abounded. The president of Moldgreen was also branch secretary of the Pressers' Union, the secretary at Rawthorpe was local secretary of the National Union of Railwaymen. The president at Deighton W.M.C. was also manager of the local Co-op., so was a member at Crosland Moor W.M.C. At election time all parties were invited to speak in the clubs, but it was rare for anyone except the Labour candidate to accept. In between elections, rooms were let at the most nominal rent for Labour Party meetings. No other parties ever asked for the space. If a club organised a tea, or had caterers in, they usually turned to the Co-op. And without exception, banked with, or borrowed from the Co-op. bank and no other. Most club statements mentioned a small number of shares in the local society. Clubs never had shares in anything else.

What, very tentatively, emerged from these observations is that the 'leaders' were leaders in a functional and in a persuasive sense. They belonged to a network of leaders throughout the working-class community. At the club responsibilities of office were well-defined, understood and respected. But responsibilities were spread widely within the club; most regular members (and the majority of members were *that*) appeared to have held minor office at some time. Control tended to be dispersed into sub-committees of real independence (as their private banking accounts show). The president and secretary held the centre steady. Like all elected officials they were involved deeply in the daily club life, and exposed to challenge and persuasion from the members at large. Deputation was never used. A club member approached his officials, as one man to one man.

Of course there were weak links. Twice we heard of absconding secretaries. Sudden, hopeless little crimes. The money easily taken, because of the way responsibility was given. But once stolen there was nothing that could be done with it—no new life away from the neighbourhood. Merely a delirious weekend at Blackpool before the police moved in.

A Male Society

'We've always had women in since Ah came here in 1919. They're sort of members now. They pay half-a-crown a year and don't have to sign in. They didn't used to be members like that—you had to sign them in every time. But it got to be a big bother, especially on Sunday nights. Ah remember they almost got to fighting in that room, did the women. We said we'd have a vote about them, and see if t'members wanted women in at all. "Nay," they all said, "If y'put your hand up to vote No, somebody's bound to tell your wife and then. . . ." "Have a *secret* ballot," Ah told them. So we had a secret ballot. Them that were scared of their wives could put in No if they wanted to. That settled it! We voted 'em out! But they started coming back again, gradually. They come in any time now. They can go anywhere except in this room, but you see them in here now at lunchtime. Ah don't bother with 'em.'

This was an old bachelor sketching one of the big changes in daily life at the club.

There was now only one club which did not admit women on to its main premises at all, but only into an adjoining concert room. This was the noisiest club ('This is the roughest part of Huddersfield—we're really in the thick of it here.'); and it had deliberately protected its maleness by having its new concert room built in such a fashion that women could enter it without intruding at all on to the club premises proper. There was still some uneasiness about women, and what they might think of gambling and drinking:

'There was a woman on Saturday night, sat over there. She was watching a fellow order his drink, and she said right out loud "That's six pints he's had: he should take that money home to his wife!" '

And there was some discomfort about sexual jokes. It wasn't that there was much of this in the clubs. There was hardly any. It was utterly unlike work: in the club you spoke much as you did at home, not as you did in the mill. Discomfort came with sex jokes at the weekend concerts: and it was, very strikingly, discomfort for the men. 'But mostly when the concert turn gets a bit near the line, it's the women that laugh out. The men just look down their noses, embarrassed mostly.'

But most clubs welcomed women, and their arrival had both increased the pleasantness of the premises and multiplied the social activities—from children's treats to fund-raising for the local gala. Being the kind of men they are, and leading daily their kind of life, the club members are equally aware of two things. On the one hand the necessary privacies and extensions of particularly masculine life that they required from their clubs, and on the other hand their obligations and indeed, yearnings, towards the world of women and children, the world of 'home'. It was this unresolved conflict which kept urging the men we spoke to, to compare their club life with 'home'. Was it another 'home' or wasn't it?

'It's like a second home here. No; it doesn't split up families—they bring their wives with 'em.'
'Ah don't make the club my home. Ah have a home of my own.'
'Look at this. It's like being at home. As long as Ah don't put me feet on the seat Ah'm all right.'

The women we met in the clubs accepted quietly this state of affairs. They readily acknowledged together with their husband's obligations to them and their family, a further private area of masculine living. Of course there were women, whom we didn't meet, who were intensely hostile to the club as a challenge to home.

'We had a member a bit since, who liked to come in and gamble a bit on his way home from work, and we got a letter from a friend of his wife saying she was threatening trouble if we didn't stop him.'

But with the increased entry of women came vastly increased

possibilities of satisfying members' feelings towards their immediate society at large. Change here had certainly enriched community.

Old Men

Much club time is given over to playing games. Cribbage and dominoes mean endless conversation and by-the-way evaluation of personalities. Spectators are never quiet, and every stage of the game stimulates comment—mostly on the characteristics of the players rather than the play; their slyness, slowness, quickness, meanness, allusions to long-remembered incidents in club history. For this no one is better equipped than the older members. They are the club's history, for it keeps no other records.

Even the most modest are full of precedent and club-lore. They have grown with the club, and their position as advisers is in no way changed by their circumstances of work. If we wanted to know anything about the club's history, the secretary would be usually at a loss to tell much, and would give way to the oldest member present: 'Nay, Ah can't tell y'owt about that. Y'want to see yond feller—he's been a member here for over fifty years.'

In some clubs this seniority was recognised more formally by altering the numbers on the membership cards each year. The member of longest standing was always number 1, and so on down the list. A slight token, but indicative of a natural turn of mind. If we happened to be in when none of the really old members were there, conversation would with deliberate calculation come round to:

'We were adding up five of their ages the other night. It did come to a sum!'

At Moldgreen, too, often our attention was drawn to the old members. On the wall were two photographs of the club committee. One taken in 1925, and the other in 1952, the club's jubilee year. They showed us that the same member appeared on both photographs: 'Look at them ears of his. Them's not right. Look like it's been taken in t'jungle. Monkeys!'

At Almondbury, there was an old man with one eye, sitting in his special place. He was eighty-three, and said this several times: and so did one or two others in the club. Round his small table were admirers; round the bar, detractors. His admirers, who included most of the women, had just given him a night out to celebrate his latest birthday. But at the bar someone said 'He says he's eighty-three, but he doesn't know. He's one of them that has three birthdays a month.' The old man was continually establishing himself by telling tales of age: 'There's a pub near Barnsley called "Hark to Mopsa" that has the oldest licensee in England. Ah said to her, "Ah'll have a pint," and she said "Sit you down, and my lad'll bring it in." He did too—and he were over eighty! She were 102 that woman.' Approval from the group. 'Nay, nay,' from a man at the bar, leaning over.

Not every member who is past retirement spends his time surrounded by a circle of admirers. The old man with one eye was rather older than most and, having been a member of *this* club only seven years, was celebrated as an acquisition. Each Friday he revisited his former club at Lindley, where he used to live. 'Ah make an afternoon and night of it. There's not many there on an afternoon, but there's one or two to talk to, and there's papers to read,' And this is how most spend their time. A few old members (and shiftworkers, and sick, and those on holiday) gather to chat, read, play games and bowls:

> 'Ah come up at ten past ten every morning and generally stay till three. Half-a-dozen or so will come in during dinner time, usually old 'uns like, there's Walt Best and that chap with the ginger hair who's just gone, and the old chap who sees the kiddies across the road at dinner-time. Steward generally shuts bar at half-past one, unless anyone comes in. We sit and talk, Ah'm last to go. He leaves me t'keys and Ah lock all up. Ah usually sit over there where you're sitting, and play with t'cat. Ah never go in a pub. Ah've only been in t'Stag Inn next door four or five times since 1919.'

In the clubs there was a *place* for age.

At the simplest level the clubs provide a change of scene for the old man, without his having to go to the silent world of the public reading room. The club is near his home and familiar. It is a part of the life of the whole society. According to energy and temperament, he may take a vigorous part in running the club. One or two officials are well over seventy. Or he may withdraw into the day-time society of those of his own age. He gets little jobs like holiday bets, locking up, or acting as doorkeeper on concert night. At Christmas he might get a special present ('fruit and cigarettes and a bottle or two'). If he's ill the club will send him to a convalescent home. His subscription is waived, or else he is formally noted an 'honorary'[1] member. The club will provide him with services, which he feels to be his earned right. The pressures upon him are slight. The club is a strand of continuity when the stable routine of work breaks down. Rather than disrupting the family relationship, it seems that the club serves to help the old member to readjust himself to the sudden increase of leisure time. Some could not readily imagine an existence without their visits to the club.

> 'What would Ah do if there wasn't t'club? Ah've nothing but home —Ah should have to stop at home and just sit by t'fire. There's TV but Ah don't watch it an hour a week; it's poor stuff on.'

In terms of daily living, such clubs differ from anything that can be externally planned for this community.

Rehousing

> 'All their social life's gone. They've got to start all over again getting a new social life. They've moved our members over to Almondbury and Newsome, and there's people from there coming over here. It's all uprooting people out, but Ah suppose nobody thinks of that.'
> (A member of Lindley Working Men's Club)

> 'On the larger housing estates an area in the neighbourhood centre is allocated for shops, church, and licensed premises.'
> (A letter we received from the Town Clerk)

From town-planning and the rehousing of long-established communities, comes the greatest danger of losing almost unseen, the traditions and social ties built up and supported by the clubs. From the town centre people are moved out to new estates, graded according to their relative 'roughness'. In the smaller communities along the valleys the stone houses are coming to the end of their

---

[1] Honorary membership really does carry the sense of being an 'honour', a recognition of service. This was recently illustrated by Nab W. M. C. who made Father Trevor Huddleston, a member for some years, into an Honorary life member, on his leaving the district. (He lists them as his club in *Who's Who*.)

useful lives. From here also people are shifted to the estates, which fill in the last pockets of farming land. All the distances involved— though small to a car-owning middle class—seem sufficient to break up the old community life.

Our first lead into this kind of problem came from conversation in Lindley W.M.C. Lindley is an old part of the town. Near the club stands an early-established Methodist Chapel, and the last-century Mechanics' Institute. The area is being demolished in stages. There is some rehousing close by:

> 'They've shifted ten of our young members right over the other side of town. They were good clubmen too, and they needn't have gone. All the Corporation had to do was to extend this estate up here a bit further, and they could have lived there. As it is they've been up-rooted out, and all their social life's gone. They've got to start all over again getting a new social life. They don't settle down again as easily once they've been uprooted out. It's all uprooting people out, but Ah suppose nobody thinks of that.'

What the speaker objects to is not, altogether, the simple loss of members, so much as the wasting of this 'social capital'. Housing shifts involve distances of only a few miles, so that at first glance it might seem that members who wished to come back could do so as often as they liked. But a few miles is a big and costly difference to a working man, who looks on distance in his own way. And clubs are anyway, not places to make a 'trip' to—like a pantomime. You casually drop into the pub on your way home from work, or back from the shops, or stroll there with the dog on an evening. By their nature, they have, for most working people, to be a few minutes away only. At first, ties are not completely broken, particularly in special circumstances. At Lindley there was a member who was a spastic:

> 'He could never work, so we made him a free member—he can come in when he likes. (He was watching the bowls). He's had to move miles away, but he still comes back here every Friday.'

Friday is a specially good night for these visits—we found several old men who revisited their former clubs then, even though they had lived in a new part of the town for some years. But most members, inevitably, stop coming. Sometimes, by an accident of development, the new housing estate may be near to a long-established community, with its own working men's club. The club members from the estate quickly join the club, and re-settle into the familiar pattern.

'Ah were up at Deighton one Thursday night, and they said to me "Not a bad turn-out for mid-week". Ah said, "No: you've got about a dozen of our old lot here." '

But even the luckiest and largest of the old clubs cannot meet the needs of a big estate built up around them.

We received a letter from the Town Clerk explaining the official view on the planning aspects of working men's clubs.

'On the larger estates an area in the neighbourhood centre is allocated for shops, churches and licensed premises. The last mentioned could be in the form of a working men's club or a public house, but we have not, I understand, had any applications for the establishment of clubs.

'The borough architect points out that working men's clubs are usually well established and do not rely on the immediately surrounding area for members who travel quite long distances to the club which attracts them.

'The main point however, is that the Corporation would be quite prepared to consider any applications received for the establishment of working men's clubs on housing estates, but they expect the initiative to come from the club people themselves.'

It is well-meant, and yet an illustration of the gap between the planning authorities and the community for which they plan. The popularity of long-established clubs near the estates show how they are needed, and how more are needed. 'Club people' will not come so easily from estates which, however fine the houses, have been thrown together from all the old districts. Brewing interests are not likely to ignore the vacant site near 'the neighbourhood centre'. The characteristic public house—which has been built on almost all the new estates—is not there to stimulate the kind of social living that we have been dealing with. Of the 'Tom Brown Inn' on one new estate a man said: 'It's not a good place. It's very new and bright and it's got a dance-floor. Everybody sits round it, and nobody knows what to do with it. It's what you'd call "jolly". No mellowness. The landlord's on the make—raking it in.'

It tells you something of the wide degree of dissociation in

British society that so little is known about working men's clubs.[1]
With over two million members, the clubs may exercise a far more
immediate influence on working-class behaviour and standards
than for example, the more conspicuous co-operative societies, or
the daily press. The clubs remain as organisations of working men,
embodying, strengthening, and passing on their style of living.
They are little touched by the mass media, little noticed by the
upper sections of society.

They have come a vast distance since the days when eleven
Dukes dipped in their pockets and Lady Stanley presided over tea
in the Deanery. A middle-class temperance crusade has been
transformed into a system of working-class drinking clubs. The
movement has little political edge, it is not concerned with any
great social causes. It has no literature, no public presence. And
yet these Huddersfield clubs illustrate what has been made out of
the hard life of industrial cities. The clubs help transform the
kinship groups into neighbourhood groups, and from a basis of
relaxation and pleasure serve innumerable human needs in a community under common pressures of accident, age, and that sudden
drop into deprivation which the working-class household fears
and seldom forgets. It is, given its cramped and modest scale, a
real achievement within a style of living. But it belongs to that
huge stretch of working-class life that exists below the 'public'
level. Sadly, this means that however fine the 'social capital', it can
be erased casually and unintentionally by the well-trained, well-
meaning middle-class man or woman who takes the decisions that
alter our landscape and our life.

[1] For a quite contradictory analysis to that offered here, see Dennis, N.,
Henriques, F., and Slaughter, C., *Coal is Our Life* (Eyre and Spottiswoode,
1956). The following quotations give the approach: 'There is little provision
for "intellectual" interests in the club . . . there are no libraries . . . there is
no "widening of horizons".' 'The means of "social intercourse" are certainly
provided, and there is a certain amount of "mutual helpfulness" but the
clubs can scarcely be said to be seriously concerned with either "mental and
moral improvement" or "rational recreations".' 'Abstractions scarcely
appear . . . there is a "Best Room" in which the conversation ranges more
widely . . . there is a strong tendency to suppress by ridicule any attempt at
differentiation.' Though the clubs fall far short by the standards applied here,
such direct pictures as the authors present, curiously speak against this kind of
judgment—as in the case of the workman who gave his friend his only pair of
glasses: 'I want you to put them in your pocket.'

Chapter Five

IN THE MILL

Written by Dennis Marsden

Focusing In

On a foggy day, the district of Aggbridge, lying in the bottom of the valley, is blotted out by the smoke from its thirty mill chimneys. The black buildings can look dreary enough. But on a fine summer day the yellow and brown stone shows through its soot covering. In the dinner hour mill-workers flock out into the streets, so that anyone not wearing a dark blue overall is out of place. Here and there in the millyards there are quick games of football; men and women sit on walls by the river, or squat on their heels in the sun talking and watching.

Tea-time is not so leisurely. There is a rush for buses. Some men can spare a few minutes for a pint before they go home. Under their dirty fawn raincoats they still wear dark blue overalls with trousers perhaps a bit too short, showing the turn-ups of a brown or grey striped suit made of that indestructible worsted which was a staple product of local mills between the wars. About half the men wear cloth caps, but these are not so popular with the young. Indoors, men can be seen through the windows sitting in shirt sleeves at their tea. Women bring their babies out on the steps to look at the workmen passing, and to watch for their husbands. In a small corner shop the daughter just home from grammar school serves on, still dressed in the shirt and tie and red skirt of her school uniform.

By the bus-stop a crowd of people sit inside a fish and chip shop, not buying anything, passing the time of day with the old man there. Half-a-dozen West Indian girls come running, with a gangling motion, laughing and jostling each other for a seat on the stone slabs of a low wall; their clothes are the same dusty colours that the local women wear. Men in the queue look on, not saying anything, but when the bus comes they are alert to prevent queue-jumping. The bus conductor has been on this route at this time for many years and knows his 'customers' intimately: 'There y'are y'old bugger. Ah've been waiting for thee. Hurry up: Ah've gett'n thee a job as a neet-watchman.'

Mill

Gradually smaller mills have had to close down, or they have been bought out by larger combines. Cartwrights, the mill of this chapter, is the biggest in this part of Huddersfield, employing over 2,000 people in good times. They once made a suit from wool, freshly sheared from a sheep, in two and a half hours: a 'world record' for twenty years. The mill is an aggregate of five smaller companies, each of which specialised in a single textile process. It still retains the character of these separate sections, and the office building carries brass plates with engraved names of the original companies.

The canal cuts through the centre of the mill, with a lock next to the warehouse, but the lockgates have gone and canal water now spills over concrete weirs. In the canal, there is filmy blue-green water, the bottom visible at the edges, ripples from fish rising to catch small white flies, rocks and debris, rusting iron bars, the upward curve of two springs from a pram carriage, and just visible below the surface, an old skep basket, crushed and disintegrating. A side road comes across the valley at right angles, twisting through between the different buildings of the mill. Here and there, lanes lead off into a dye-house or a large yard; but some buildings are sited awkwardly and men have to climb down from loading bays six feet above the ground if they want to fetch tea from the canteen by the shortest route. There are pleasanter roads into the mill, stony cart-tracks leading down from the main road past small mill-ponds set among trees, and some people come to work this way; but the main flow is down the hill and over the canal bridge, where at dinner-time a woman from the local shop brings a basket of fish and chips to sell.

Each mill has a striking square water-tower, Victorian, on the lines of a mediaeval castle turret. One mill-building is very much like another, with regular rows of windows, seldom cleaned, and little architectural decoration. But more important to the workpeople are the irregular nooks and crannies and the lavatories. These are the meeting-places on which much of the mill's informal social life depended.

Finishing Shed

This chapter is based on the finishing shed, a single-storey, glass-roofed building. The shed is several very large 'rooms', more or less divided up by walls, passageways or rows of machines. In two, the machines were all operated by men. Their work is 'wetting out' the cloth to shrink it, 'blowing' and 'tentering' or drying, 'mosering' (raising the pile), and 'cutting' the long fibres on the cloth. Other machines press, steam and brush, or 'nap' it, raising small loops on its surface. This is the 'finishing' room from which the cloth goes straight to 'perchers', who look at it for faults and return unsatisfactory pieces, perhaps to be rebrushed or even to go through the whole finishing process again.

The largest central room mixed kinds of work, skilled and unskilled. All along one side were 'perches' where rolled and folded cloth was skewered together into a continuous flow, and fed through holes in the ceiling to the perchers in the room above. The men on this simple job of skewering are called 'tail-enders', a generic term for all those men doing the less skilled part of a two-man job with a skilled man—the 'head-ender'. The middle of the floor was taken up by 'scrays', flat upturned metal boxes arranged in rows with just enough room between them for carts to pass. Upon these scrays were piled the rolled and folded pieces of cloth brought in from other processes. At one end of the shed 'menders' were grouped close together at tilted tables like drawing boards on which cloth was spread. These girls and women repaired faults in the cloth or coloured it up with chalks to make it look an even shade. Next to them, and down the side of the room were cutting, brushing-and-steaming, and pressing machines with men doing heavy work on piece-rates. By each machine was a price list worked out by the management which stated the wage rates for work done on that machine in units calculated to two decimal places of a penny. It was impossible to judge the shape of this room. Its walls were hidden by machines, which stretched away under arches or concealed recesses leading to other rooms, so that there were many dark corners. In an exit passageway hung yellow-ing, minutely-printed notices of the Factory Acts and First Aid Instructions.

In summer, working conditions were unpleasant. The glass roof-windows were seldom opened and the cooling fans were never switched on, so that in a heat-wave with machines giving off clouds of steam, the heat and humidity rapidly rose above the prescribed standard. Some machines cut and pulled fibres from the cloth, and this 'flock', which is injurious to health, should have been sucked away from each machine by a large nozzle leading to an overhead air main. Damp flock often clogged together, and much of it finished up on the floor round the machine, to be swept up continually by a very slowly moving workman with heart-disease, who brushed his way round the shed, week in, week out.

Lavatories

Because they were the only places where a man could reasonably expect to be free from the surveillance of authority, the lavatories occupied a unique place in the mill's social life. Smoking was officially prohibited and there was no provision for men to meet for a five-minute break, so that lavatories became the unofficial smoking room. They were labelled 'MALES', and within range of the finishing shed there were two. One inside the shed was a nub and centre of social life, with up to twenty men there at un-officially 'recognised' break-times. It was a long, high narrow room with a row of ten W.C.s down one side, each in its own wooden cubicle, and a urinal at one end. Those W.C.s not actually in use formed seats for some men who propped the doors open so that they could talk to friends squatting against tiled walls opposite or leaning against the wooden partitions. Floor and guttering were always littered with cigarette butts and match-stalks. The once-white tiles were thickly stained with dark brown nicotine from tobacco smoke.

In summer men felt the need of a 'breath of fresh air' and a look at the weather outside. Then they went to a lavatory in the mill yard, where they could meet men from the weaving and spinning sections of the mill. By chance, just outside this lavatory was a small patch of ground in an angle between two buildings. It was screened from the yard and the view of passing officials by a large buttress. It was a draughty, smelly, dusty corner at the best of times, where large black smuts often fell from a nearby chimney. Here someone had made a crude seat with a plank across two irregular knobs of concrete.

There were two other meeting-places. The canteen was used by about half the work-people, and it was the occasion for friends to sit together rather than for meeting newcomers. Every area of this canteen had its own intimate groups, apparently quite haphazardly seated, but really strictly defined. A new man, early in for dinner at an empty table, was warned, 'You don't want to sit there; you'll be among t'women.' After dinner in the large mill yard other steady groups sat on window ledges or bales of shoddy, or they squatted on their heels against walls of buildings, eyeing the men and girls as they walked back to work, some of them eating ice-cream. 'Look at yond feller wi' t' black coat' (a West Indian with very long hair). 'See that on a dark night and you wouldn't half run!' 'We've gett'n a new flapper. That's a short skirt in't it. If it were any shorter she'd be showing all she's got.' There were always one or two men, like the man who stands at the public bar, who preferred to harangue rows of seated men from a standing position, never quite joining any group.

Community

Cartwrights as a whole was not a 'community' in any simple sense. The urge towards a closer life together flickered and spurted up here and there, sometimes strongly. But this group of one hundred or so men and women who worked in and around the finishing shed was shot through by diversions which were deep, although they seldom appeared on the surface.

Outwardly all was friendly and intensely physical in an uninhibited way. Men touched each other very readily: all over there were mock fights and practical jokes, with wrestling, men putting up fists and patting bald heads, offers to buffet, jostle or trip anyone who came within reach. In quiet conversation the urge was to touch, draw aside by an elbow, rest a hand on a shoulder, or simply to lean close. There was an absent-minded quality in the way men worked, waiting for distractions, eager to seize any excuse for a laugh and a joke. Work became second nature and the mill's bustling life proceeded, with work as the reason for men's presence but not their main concern. Some simple jobs were performed by men described as 'simple'. But this equation of intellectual capacity with work did not hold in the majority of jobs, where the only satisfaction offered by work was a task such as rolling a piece of cloth neatly so that the end of the roll should be flat.

Noise was a severe handicap on some machines, which rendered conversation difficult at normal distances until men had learned to lip-read a little and to give to their voices a penetrating tone so that they could speak without strain. There was a knack, too, in avoiding fatigue from gazing too long at cloth streaming over rollers or along waving arms before it fell into natural folds. Watching this was a sure way to induce sleep. Jobs were ostensibly tied down to one machine, but new work brought in from other departments was dumped with no particular system on the scrays, so that there was a constant circulation of men looking for pieces. These pieces had to be piled on stout wooden carts searched out from all parts of the finishing shed, as they were emptied by other men. There was the trip to find the foreman, to the stores, to the water-tap. Tea was brought round twice a day, and there was a queue at the urn. And above all there were the lavatories which were full of talking men two or three times each morning, and perhaps twice in the afternoon. Everybody might get to know, casually or intimately as he chose, almost all the men and women, boys and girls working in and around the finishing shed. 'It's like coming back home. I know three-quarters of this lot,' said a man who had been away at another mill for five years. Anyone coming through on 'business' was hailed from each machine and passing girls ran a gauntlet of friendly enquiries and embraces.

Common knowledge included a man's most intimate private affairs, especially if, as often happened, more than one member of a family worked in the mill. 'He worries a lot. And he's got his mother and father living with him, and his wife's mother. And his daughter's slipped up, as you might say. Her husband, well he's not her husband but the one 'at were going to marry her backed out and she's pregnant. And I shouldn't be surprised if t'baby weren't black when it's born. She's been going round a long time with 'em. She works in that Pakistani restaurant down Mission Street. And her father wouldn't harm a fly. He's one o' t' nicest men you could wish to meet, a strong Baptist, or he used to be. . . .' The main tenor of these relationships was friendliness, but not blandness. Shrewd judgments informed many jokes and comments. It didn't take long to learn that 'yon woman on number three perch is a bad bugger; she doesn't want to do any work', or that 'you could have a row with that man on t'next machine in two minutes if you didn't watch out'. A man over-eager to create about him an atmosphere of intense activity was soon placed by: 'Aye, he does a lot of *talking* does Charlie.'

Men came from different districts up and down the valleys, and birthplace became at once a link and a point of difference: 'We'll have to get somebody to come and talk to thee i' Dunthwaite because you don't seem to understand what *we* say. Shall we get James Shaw to come and talk to you i' Dunthwaite and try and make you understand?' 'Why, is James Shaw a Dunthwaiter then?' 'You live in Dunthwaite and you don't know who lives there?' 'Ah, that's a different thing from being a *Dunthwaiter*—living there. Y'have to be three generations living there before you're a Dunthwaiter.' 'Well, if I lived i' Dunthwaite I should keep it dark, it's nowt to be proud on. . . .' And so on; there were endless variations on this line of banter.

Such conversation was no more than an opening; tentative gestures towards a relationship. And with some men relationships at work could harden at this level—joking could be a barrier, exclusive as well as inclusive in its workings. Since the need for a good laugh was almost a compulsion, time and time again conversation was led away from a central topic by a listener who seized an opening for an easy joke. But for most men these asides had the function of keeping open the flow of a relationship where conversations could often last only a few seconds in passing.

Swearing and sexual conversation bound the men together. As a topic on which most men could support a conversation and as a source of jokes, sexual talk and gesture were inexhaustible. In the machine noise a gesture suggestive of masturbation, inter-course or homosexuality was enough to raise a conventional smile and re-establish a bond over distances too great for talking. It was questionable how far such comment sprang from the quality of a man's life and feelings. It would be impertinent, on the strength of only an hour or two's conversation with a man to say anything on this point. But, as with joking, so with 'sex'; the conditions of life in the mill were such that some men's need for a quick joke or sexual remark became almost compulsive. Sex came and went in conversation with scarcely a variation in tone of voice or manner: a man looking at a spindle would say, as the thought bubbled up, 'Just do for a woman to frig herself off with, wouldn't it?' Sometimes the tone was superficial, and when such thinking became an insistent end in itself a man was so much the less respected, even by men who might laugh at his remarks.

Swearing went with all kinds of other diversions and habits, and a man could soon sense by this tone in conversation where his affinities lay. The 'quiet' person who did not swear was not unknown nor unrespected—although 'respect' in this context does not necessarily convey a sense of the superior morality of the non-swearer, so much as a 'live-and-let-live' adjustment on the part of the man he was talking to. Swearing had an inclusive and exclusive character; in certain of the groupings it was *essential* to swear, and to swear 'correctly', for a man to be included as an intimate: 'What you tired for? You fucking too hard? No? Why you never say anything, make me laugh?' A need to swear was felt by some who had to emphasize their manhood. But apart from this it could indicate other kinds of separation and desires to belong. Three of the men who swore frequently in a way which attracted attention were a Pole, a West Indian, and a former grammar school boy who had a precarious position one stage above manual work.

Equally, swearing could actively exclude a man from a group by pointing to his difference, even to his 'unmanliness'. Deliberately exclusive behaviour would, perhaps, have to be provoked by some other marks of foreignness beyond a sexual weakness. One student who worked at the mill during his college vacation succeeded in getting himself accepted by adopting a dialect accent, and by carefully following the leads on swearing and grumbling which the men threw out. But another set out to emphasise that he was no workman. 'He used to come every day with his umbrella. Dick asked him "Are y'courtin' Raymond?" and he said he was, and Dick said, "Have you shagged her yet?" and Raymond says "Good gracious no!" just like that, "Good gracious no!" So Dick says, "Oh, that's no good. You want to get her shagged." And he couldn't bear swearing. He used to put his hands over his ears when he heard them at it. Of course, when the lads found out he couldn't stand swearing they went at it much worse! As hard as they could.'

Foreman and Management

The 'community' was very broad, spilling over and embracing any workmen who came along from another part of the mill. But there was a severely defined upper limit—it did not include the shed manager, James Shaw, or his under-manager, Fred Beaumont. These two men were nearly always accorded the dignity of their full names, in contrast with the rest of the workmen who were known by their Christian names and their machines, and only by their full names as a last resort. These two managers, or foremen, had, apparently, been men of ability who had once been part of the body of workmen in the shed, doing semi-skilled work. 'You know about James Shaw, do you? Came from a poor family—they're not poor now mind, but they were at one time. He used to work on t'steamer, and then he got the job Fred Beaumont has now, and then he got this job. And Fred Beaumont was on t'steamer too, and he was going to leave and they called him in and made him foreman just like that, no qualifications, although he knows a bit about it does Fred.'

James Shaw had climbed out of the immediate level of manual workmen, and in extremely hot weather he sometimes took off his jacket, but never his tie or his waistcoat. Fred Beaumont still felt very keenly the scrutiny of former workmates—he was here, there and everywhere with a worried frown which seldom relaxed —and he never appeared without the thick dark blue jacket of his serge suit, even during a heat-wave when sweat was obviously pouring from him. 'He's never had that coat off for three years! When he first came in here you couldn't get a word out of him— he'd too much on his mind. At first t'job got on top of him.' Recently the *Huddersfield Examiner* reported that a man in this position had hanged himself from a beam in the weaving shed. James Shaw could allow himself to joke 'as an equal' with men and women, to the extent of being told by one workman 'now don't be cheeky'. Fred Beaumont could never allow any familiarity, and preserved a great sternness.

As James Shaw got higher he became associated with the superstructure of clerical workers who 'did nothing', and it was rumoured that he 'wouldn't last long': Fred Beaumont was 'doing all the work' and 'carrying' him. There was a general dislike and mistrust of clerical workers and minor officials who came through the shed to examine the cloth, speaking to no one below the level of foreman. 'See that feller there. No qualifications, failed his 'City and Guilds' about eleven times, but since he's got that job he'll hardly speak to you. Ah'd get rid of him if I were t'manager o' this place. The trouble with this place is there are too many non-producers. It all started wi't'last manager. Take t'managing director. Well, he has an assistant. Fair enough, all right, he *deserves* an assistant, he's a busy man. But that *assistant* has an assistant, and *he's* got an assistant. That's how it goes on at this place. There's a new one every week in a white coat.'

But these 'clerical' workers were hardly sufficiently established to become a corporate hostile body of 'them'. Management was too far away and too diffuse in its workings to be resented for much other than its anonymity and distance.

The Disabled

Disablement was an everyday fact of working in the mill. At the corner by the foreman's office sat a pretty, crippled girl, perching and mending. The man who swept up had heart disease; a man who brought round the tea urn had only one good arm and managed the tap with a rubber stump on an artificial metal arm. A minor accident threw up a whole crop of reminiscences from men in the shed, of accidents to themselves or to near relatives; of broken bones, torn limbs, bad burns; cases of people who had been rendered incapable of doing their skilled work, so that they had to spend the rest of their working lives labouring. Regardless of bodily weakness or incapacity a man had to work, employing his diminished skills as best he could. All these disabled people were working side by side with strong men doing heavy work.

There was a similar, less easily perceived gradation from heavy, fast jobs, to lighter, less well paid but slower and less variable work. Some really heavy, rushed processing was done by muscular boys of under twenty, who took a pride in physically matching up to older men: 'You can't come to work half asleep on this job.' One older man characterised these processes as 'young men's work' compared with his own 'nice steady job'.

Some of the strength and weakness of this mill 'community' is revealed in its attitude towards mental illness. There was room for a mentally ill person if he or she could do a job of work efficiently. A large, strong man who had worked at the mill for many years had a very pronounced nervous stammer and a tick which often compelled him to stop and perform ritualistic motions with his hands. A young boy, with mild epilepsy, had fits of complete blankness when for several seconds he had no idea where he was. Both of them did labouring jobs, and they had worked at the mill long enough to be accepted without comment, except for well-intentioned jokes from intimate friends.

But the 'simple' or mentally ill person might fall a victim to the need for a 'good laugh' promoted by the boredom of work. A girl mender, who was so deeply entangled in the fantasy world of 'pop' singers that she began to give 'concerts' in the dinner hour, drew an exceptionally large and appreciative audience. Eventually the foreman had to intervene to stop this exploitation. The instance of a mental patient called Thomas provides a richer impression of this 'tolerance' with its coarser streak of insensitivity. Thomas was a childish man who had been in a local mental hospital many times for schizophrenia. He was over sixty and he had no skills upon which to draw. An attempt was made to rehabilitate him as a 'tail-ender' on the perches, but during the time of this study his fate was in the balance. The perchers good-naturedly passed him on, once every three days. 'It's as much as we can stand!' And from the rest of the workmen Thomas got much good advice and banter—'Na then, how you going on, Thomas lad,'—to which he responded, very pleased. But he was over-forgetful and too fussy for the chargehand on the job, who was too dignified to fend off his clutching hands. The chargehand couldn't respond to Thomas's excited shouting and laughing with

'Get away y'old bugger', as other workmen did. Any mentally ill person who was to fit in must not only be able to do his work, but he would often have to be insensitive enough either to ignore or respond to the laughter.

Mill Trip

Occasionally people in the finishing shed were moved by a stronger urge to celebrate their friendships. Daily work was the scene of all sorts of minor gestures of friendliness—collections for 'him in t'corner that's getting married a Sat'day', or offers to mind another man's machine for him or help him with a heavy piece. In part of the finishing shed, people who had worked together for a long time were organising a mill trip (there were several) whose moving impulse was to unite work with the world of home. 'That other do's not t'sort of a trip you can take a woman on' (i.e. a woman *relative*), 'so we're having a trip of us own in here, one that you can take your wife and I can take my girl-friend. It were Ronnie's idea, and he asked me first, and I said yes, and he asked them across there and they'll come, and them two Poles over on t'perch, they'll come with their wives. You see them two foreigners over there, they'll not come; they don't like spending their money.'

The friendliness which was outwardly all-embracing didn't knit all the mill workers together. The trip which was to express their friendships excluded the women who worked alongside the organisers—with whom they were, apparently, on the friendliest terms—as being much coarser and more insensitive than the wives and girl-friends who couldn't be taken on the management's mill trip. And foreigners were selected very carefully from the most skilled workmen. At this point where the urge to draw together was strongest, divisions of sex and nationality cracked open the friendly surface.

Mill Girls

The women working alongside men added an extra dimension to life in the finishing shed. There was no resentment between them on the grounds of work, for overlapping was only slight. Traditionally women had always worked in the mills, and during the

last war women had been trained as perchers, but otherwise jobs
in this department went strictly by sex, since much of the men's
work was heavy and demanded strength enough to lift a piece
single-handed. A keen political consciousness was needed to make
the difficult analysis which saw women as a fundamental cause of
the depressed condition of textile wages: 'That's why people in
the valley are all Socialists. Things have been very bad in the
valley all the time. I mean that they've been so bad that women
have had to go out to work, and I think that's a shameful thing
myself. And I think it's a bad thing as well, because if women
hadn't gone out to work I think they'd have had to do something
about the wages and they'd have been higher than they are now.
They're the worst wages there are, and the longest hours.' Women
were such a familiar part of the everyday scene that no one at
Cartwrights ever expressed this economic hostility (the comment
is from a man farther up the valley), but such feelings may have
lain deep below the more obvious sexual harshness.

At best, the presence of girls and women could bring a constant
reminder of home and the outside community. It gave the working
society a kind of completeness, even a hint of children and
regeneration on a plane quite other than that of the constant
flow of sexual jokes. One young mender was five months pregnant. She had started work straight from school, 'a little slip of a
thing', and a man who was now her husband used to work at
Cartwrights. 'They got to going out odd nights, and they got
on a bit farther, and I suppose they must have got to sleeping
together. Anyway, they got married last week. She were five
months gone and she's only sixteen.' This girl was never the
object of any sexual jokes. Her condition was a topic of daily and
absorbing interest to the men, who would remark on how tired
or pale she looked. The women menders helped with her work—
she came to work out of necessity in the rush of setting up a
home. Since she was on a fixed rate they could perform all kinds
of minor jobs for her which lightened the work, and if she
sometimes slept, her hands resting on the mending-board, the
chargehand ignored this. More than any other mender she was to
be seen in quiet conversation with the men, who were so keenly
interested that one of them gently ran his hand over her swelling
stomach. Her husband had been forced to leave the mill by

pressure of a corporate opinion which still welled up when she looked particularly ill: 'He ought to have the baby rammed down his fucking throat.'

But this dimension of home and children brought into work tensions which could never be fully resolved. Men were much more embarrassed than women in discussing sex in mixed company outside work. Sexual joking belonged essentially to a male society, to work rather than home, for under the scrutiny of women it became something not real, even debasing. So men never used sexual swear-words at home—'Ah know some men speak to their girl-friends like that, but Ah wouldn't speak to mine that way. She's not the type.' Nor did close male relatives swear sexually in each other's presence.

Cartwrights couldn't be divided neatly into separate groups of each sex, because men and women might work on adjacent machines or they were able to shout across intervening distance. And the element of mime in many sexual jokes meant that distance didn't lend a reassuring privacy. These conditions induced a sort of bravado, where men enjoyed the possibilities of innuendo in joking with women. But the very fact that these possibilities existed point to the nervousness of men who were trespassing against traditional ideals of womanly purity and, at a deeper level, the securities of family life. A younger man came to work dressed all in black and his new outfit brought a comment from a middle-aged woman minder. 'What you all in black for today? I don't like you in black.' 'T'cat's died. It makes me look more muscular when I'm dressed in black.' 'Where?' 'A*ha*!' On another occasion two men in high spirits caught each other's eye; and behind a piece of cloth which was hanging like a curtain, blocking them, as they thought, from the menders' view, a quick-mimed sexual joke passed between them. They found they had been seen by two menders and dissolved into laughter while one of the men mouthed across to the women, 'Filthy, that man, filthy!' They enjoyed this bond established with the women, and a friend went across to get the menders' comments, 'They say all you can do is *talk* and *think* about it nowadays.' 'Who says so? We'll show them. We'll take them out tonight, you and me Jim, in the car, eh? You coming out with us tonight?' (he shouted across to the women) 'Lindley Moor, lots of fresh air!'

There is a slight queasiness about these exchanges. Men have
their eyes on their fellow workmen, for the invitation to these
women to join the male society was not genuine: if a woman
accepted sexual joking and conversation at the men's level she
immediately lost their respect. A man who one minute said, 'See
that over there—she's a common thing. I bet she's 'f'ing and
blinding now', could be joking rather contemptuously with the
same girl a moment later: 'She said, "Have you got a match?" I
said "Yes, your face and my arse." It's not very original I
know. . . .' Between the sexes, as between men themselves, subtle
grades of swearing defined a relationship. A woman percher
thought the men were 'a decent lot' who swore like any men did,
'but they know when to use it and who to use it with'. And there
were other hints of different groupings among the women: 'We've
had all sorts working here. This isn't a bad place, mills are all the
same. We had a couple of prostitutes working here once—well,
they didn't do it all t'time. T'other women told us. They told
t'women and t'women told t'men. None of t'women would use
toilets when them two were here. But Larry asked a doctor and
he said VD's not infectious.'

The guilt associated with drawing women into the men's world
transferred itself to women mill-workers in general. In a complex
way never clearly expressed, men felt that mill work was de-
grading for women: a judgment which carries overtones of
self-disgust, for if men felt that the women from Cartwrights
were in some way tainted, the taint was that of their own
men's world. This opens the way to a partial understanding
of the tales of sexual 'orgy' which always poured out when mill
trips were recalled. One young organiser of an informal mill
trip remembered a trip two years before, when he was sixteen.
The occasion left him more experienced, but at the expense of
a deeply-rooted mistrust of girls who had been with him on the
trip.

'They put all of us in t' "lollipop bus"—that's all of them who's
under eighteen, and there's no beer allowed on that bus, and you
don't get tobacco, cigarettes and that. You get some sweets instead,
and when you come back they call at a fish and chip shop instead of a
pub, but of course there was a pub just across t'road. I had a lot of
fun that trip. I enjoyed meself, although it wouldn't be what I'd call

fun now like. They have two buses, one for t'girls, and one for t'boys. That's t'way it starts off, until they stop for t'first time and then we get organised and some o' t' girls come into t'boys bus, and some o' t' boys goes into t'girls bus. By! We had some shockers used to work here three years ago. I don't think they're quite as bad now as they used to be. They're a bit more respectable, t'lot that works here now. Y'had to make your plans, sort of who you were going with. We had 'em laid out on t'back seat before we got to Blackpool. You know—shouts of "Stop it!" '

'I wouldn't like my girl friend to have to work here: not from t'work point of view, but from what they have to put up with and t'language they have to hear.' It wasn't simply a question of language, but by putting a finger on one point, this man could indicate other areas of social life. He was expressing a desire that the different worlds of home and work should remain separate. Any closer linking would require him to change his behaviour— swearing, and so on—but more fundamentally it would upset some of his basic categories of thought about women. And it was true that through hearing every day the talk and jokes of men at work, some of the girls and women had developed a fixed, slightly hard facial expression and a facility with back-chat which hinted at a growing insensitivity in their relationships with other work-people.

The conclusions and descriptions in this section must remain as very tentative suggestions only of what might go on when no observer is there. For on this topic, as well as in collecting a documentation of swearing, what people say depends even more subtly than usual on the person they are talking to. When the observer doesn't swear, he may attract respectful attention: 'I'm trying to give up swearing. I think it's just ignorance don't you? I wouldn't swear if I was talking to somebody like you for instance.' Or, more disturbingly, like the student, he can attract an impatient contempt: 'What about your mate here? He looks as though he could do with a blow-through.' 'Oh, him, he couldn't manage one. It'd kill him!' And there is the danger that more colourful, usually sexual, exchanges will obscure that steady flow of interest in the weather, gardening, the bookie's runner, 'Did you bowl last night then, Stanley?'—which is so much more difficult to pin down.

Foreigners

Most of the menders lived in Aggbridge. The mill was always understaffed in this department so women could work part-time near to their homes. But many of the men came from other villages, or even from small towns ten miles away on the other side of the city. Over half the workers in the finishing shed were Poles or Latvians, who had begun to arrive in the city over ten years ago. There was now a sprinkling of West Indian men in the finishing shed and elsewhere in the mill, and a few West Indian girls worked in the weaving department.

Splits in the working population showed up most clearly in the mill yard during the fifteen minutes or so which followed dinner in the canteen. Half-a-dozen West Indians sat in a very exposed position on a few large cubical bales of 'shoddy'. Down the side of the yard by the lavatory there was usually a row of 'skeps'— wickerwork baskets—which were the preserve of up to thirty Polish workers. Local men sat on the window-sills of the main office-building.

Without hypocrisy, locally-born workmen laughed and joked with Poles and West Indians, but at the same time they were hostile to 'foreigners' in general. Individual friendships did exist, as the informal mill trip illustrated; and in speaking of 'foreigners' local men made exception for 'these two over here' or 'him next to me'. But each odd taciturn, 'unfriendly' or bad-tempered 'foreigner' strengthened the hostile stereotype.

The characteristics of this 'foreigner' were difficult to plot. Depending on the subject under discussion, 'foreigners' were variously accused of talking too much or too little; 'There's some of 'em, they'll go on that works trip and they'll make a *profit* out of it; they don't spend their own money. They eat all t'meals, and drink all t'free beer, and they have a pound spending money, but they don't spend that. They go and sit on t'sand all afternoon, stingy devils!' 'They've never had any money before, a lot of 'em, but they only waste it when they get it. Spend it on silly stuff like clothes, instead of saving it up to get a home together'. They were said to have large families ('but that's their own fault'), they swore 'too much', worked too hard or were lazy . . . and so on. Prejudice fed on whatever was available.

West Indians

'What d'you think about t'colour bar then?' 'I think they should put 'em in quarantine for six months when they first come here. They're not civilised, some of 'em. I know some's all right, but they come here and they've got all sorts of uncivilised habits, living together in one house. And when you talk to 'em they're just like animals. All they can think of is sex.' This view was based on talking to one West Indian who had worked in the finishing shed for two weeks. Yet the speaker represented one section of the very responsible men encountered during the study. He was a member of a Methodist Youth Club and a brass band— a keen debater who was soon to become a leader at the club. He wasn't alone in his notions of a superior way of life. Two workmen sitting on a window-sill watching the West Indians coming back from dinner also felt the basic division, if in softer terms; 'Dosta see these Indians, t'way they walk? They lift their feet up vertically and then put 'em down on t'heel.' 'Aye, it's walking through t'jungle that does that to 'em.' 'Dosta think so.' 'Aye, climbing these 'ere mountain passes.' 'Or riding camels?'

Such opinions were deeply rooted, although in the mill's friendly atmosphere they tended to be submerged in a flow of conversation and jokes. But prejudice died hard: a young man was offering round sweets to workmen on nearby machines, when a West Indian suddenly felt the hidden barrier—'All right, I take it, but you never take fuck-all I offer you. Your hands clean?' Quite simply local workers suspected black men of being more likely to have venereal disease.

The queue for the bus each evening was another occasion for friction. West Indians had not yet submitted to the habit of queueing. They made nothing of this line of English workmen and tended to join the queue where any friend was standing. There were always arguments between white and coloured workers, who were told to 'get to the back of the queue, that's your rightful place'.

Polish Workers

Hostility towards Polish workmen was equally deep but couched in different terms. There were many more of them, and although they had been in the district for ten years or more they were older workmen near retiring age who had never managed to pick up much of the local dialect. They got along by an elaborate set of smiles, grimaces and signs, and this failure to learn local ways seems to be one of the reasons why such divisions as existed when these workers first arrived in the district had not been smoothed over. The urge towards conversation came so strongly in the local men that when it was frustrated by the wooden responses which were the best the Poles could give, there were occasional explosions of resentment. Poles with whom they could scarcely communicate laughed and joked together in a way which had an uncanny, almost wilful air of exclusiveness and unsociability. And from this is it only a short step to accusations of arrogance which any lack of deference to local custom could bring. Sometimes men came to blows: 'Here, you have a spell with this bugger, he's driving me barmy with his smiling and waving. Ah can't stand it.' An older Polish workman who spoke no English had been severely bruised in a fight with a younger man in just this situation, and only the very disturbed working conditions, where men never knew from one day to the next whom they would work with, prevented more fights. If two workmen teamed up for a longer period, they were always of the same nationality.

So much for surface hostility: but there were deeper undercurrents of resentment which drew their bitterness from the losing battle fought by textile workers against employers. When the Poles arrived in the district union activity was at a low ebb. Recently the management of Cartwrights had been able to do more or less what it wanted in the way of rate-fixing, overtime, working conditions, and all those other areas of working life normally protected by union agreement. The owner was of central European origin—none of the workmen was very clear as to which country—and he had 'looked after his own' so far as to encourage Polish workers to come to Cartwrights. There was no union activity in the finishing shed. Men were very discontented with working conditions and rates of pay, and this resentment fixed on the Poles. The older workmen saw things in a clearer perspective: 'There used to be a lot of little unions, there were the "Dyers and Finishers", that were a good 'un. At one time you couldn't get a job here without a union card. But they went down. They've never had the leaders they should have had; they never recovered from the 1920s. That's what finished it. These foreigners aren't interested in unions. T'Poles haven't made t'place any better. We used to have our own practices—we never worked over on Friday night, however busy we were. We always had Friday night off, but when they came they wanted to work Fridays, so that were that.' But to younger men, some of whom hadn't the textile workers' sense of history engrained in their working lives, the Poles appeared as the causers of decay rather than its attenders. 'There's too many foreigners at this place for my liking. Not that I've got anything against 'em personally—I get on well with 'em—but they're too greedy. Look, if you said to that feller there "Will you work over tonight and through till tomorrow morning, and then work over tomorrow night again", he'd do it.' 'Even if they're ten shillings short in their pay-packets they never complain. I don't know what they're frightened of.'

The Polish workers in their shut-off, seemingly deferential, concentrated application to their work were a nullification of the 'ideal' working community.

Change

How typical was Cartwrights; and why did men and women work there, rather than anywhere else? A study taken over only four weeks must, of necessity, be tentative on all these points. But they were so insistently a part of 'work' that to leave the study without locating Cartwrights' finishing shed in this frame of reference would be misleading.

The *Huddersfield Examiner* reports in its annual trade review that 'the general conception that the textile industry is not quite up to its competitors in social status is now realised to be a serious handicap in attracting suitable labour'. 'Status' is the wrong word to describe the past struggles of the textile workers and their relationships to workers in other industries. During the Luddite riots a local mill owner was murdered by his workmen and until times easily within living memory the mill owners have been a legend for meanness. Sir Isaiah Haigh stopped a sum equivalent

to the new old age pension from the pay packets of his oldest
employees on the grounds that 'tha can't work for more na one
wage'. Men not yet turned sixty had worked under these auto-
crats, whose high-handedness had shaped the socialist consciousness of much of the valley.

> 'That mill across t'yard opposite t'office used to belong to Schofield
> Sykes. Ah can just remember him when I were a lad coming to work
> in frock coat and tails. That mill only made eight pieces a day in them
> days, eight pieces a day! But they were good worsted. Aye, and
> when he died he left two hundred and fifty thousand. Then Stoner
> Cartwright used to have it, but he were extravagant. His women
> cost him a bit. He had one or two divorce cases, and then he got
> into t'hands o' t' bank, and it's not been t'same since. He used to
> come here soused in champagne, but he knew his job though. He
> were one o'them that used to go off golfing round t'world six month
> out o' t' year, and then he'd come back and start. He'd sack a couple
> of managers straight away, just to cause a bit of excitement.'

Obviously, too, these mill owners commanded a grudging respect,
not only as 'characters' whose marked idiosyncrasies and physical
presence contrast with the faceless, distant bankers; but also they
'know their jobs' and they believed in work, hard work, as a
basic fact of living. One of the men doing a very minor job in a
white coat was a link with this past ideal:

> 'He's one of the original Cartwrights, there, with that coat on. Ah
> think he was a son or something, but he must have been one of the
> sort that won't learn. That were one thing about t'Cartwrights. They
> believed in hard work and anybody in t'family that were starting in
> t'mill had to start at t'bottom and work their way up to t'top; and
> they made sure that they did get to t'top mind, but he mustn't have
> wanted to learn and there it is.'

Even though the valley was a Socialist or old-style Liberal
stronghold the textile unions had never gained a bargaining hold
after strikes during the Depression. The large number of women
in the industry and the way in which their presence split the
community, may be important. Men at Cartwrights had come
from other industries, they were 'foreigners', or they were too
young to have the older men's feeling for unions. One or two saw
the weakened state of the textile industry and said, 'The union's

never done any good; why should we join?' So the unions were caught in a vicious spiral of decreasing membership. The high piece-rates paid at Cartwrights were not agreed by negotiation. There had been union officials at the mill but the last one had been sacked. And without corporate bargaining as a counter-weight to their corporate plight, other sides of community could never grow. If the textile workers were enjoying high wages it was as a result of union activity in *other* industries, where wage-rates had risen until engineering, chemical and electrical manufacturing firms threatened to draw away the city's work-men.

The textile industry stood at a greater disadvantage in the trade cycles than other local industries, which were expanding almost without pause. Textiles were still subject to alarming and un-predictable fluctuations. The mysterious quality of these trade cycles had gone deep into local minds:

> 'Why, it's no wonder trade's not so good. Has ta seen where t'girls and t'women have gett'n their coats and dresses. They don't come below their knees, some of 'em. Some o' t' lasses is freetened to sit da'en. Ah remember t'last time women's fashions were like this, when we had t'slump in 1930, that were.'

Cartwrights had been forced by competition from Europe to go over to the highly seasonal trade of weaving fabrics for women's coats—'ladies' coats' as they were called in the mill. Less cloth was used for the summer coats and it did not require as much 'finishing'. So the finishing sheds were extremely short of men during summer—when the winter cloths were woven—but greatly under-employed in winter, with short time for some men and no piece-rates for the majority.

Perhaps only the 'boom' conditions at Cartwrights made this study possible. West Indians had only recently been introduced into the finishing shed because the need for workmen there had overcome all the management's fears ('These were t'words: "Get some bloody men in that finishing shed whatever the colour of their skins" '). Cartwrights offered no guarantee that an em-ployee would be found work after the summer, or that he would not be laid off. They compensated for this by offering high piece-rates in an attempt to attract floating workmen for the rush of work. Side by side with men who had worked at the same mill all their lives were others who had been there only a day, a few weeks, or a year. And these were often not young men, just starting work: they were part of a floating group who 'felt like a change after five years or so'. In the canteen at meal-times those men who had worked at the mill for a few years always sat at the same tables with a group of friends. But there were men from the finishing shed who sat alone, behind the barrier of a newspaper. One of these had started work in his home village thirty years ago, but he had left after a row with the foreman. Ever since he had drifted about trying many different jobs, a quiet man who had aroused a friendly response but made no lasting friendships at work. Before working at Cartwrights he had been working on the buses for five years; then at a local engineering works. After four years at Cartwrights he was again ready for a move. Among the younger men was an apprentice electrician, too young to receive full trade pay in his own trade, who wanted to earn some quick money to get married. A salesman, laid off during the hire purchase restrictions, stood out because of a blandness in his approach and his over-readiness to point out how new he was to manual work.

Other parts of the mill didn't suffer such fluctuations: 'Ah think it's only in t'finishing it's like this. It's different in t'scouring. Ah seems to get on right well with 'em in there. They're different jobs—there's not as much money. There don't seem to be as many foreigners there, one or two Irish, that's all.' At this time Cartwrights was a melting-pot, the resort of workers newly arrived in the district, or of men who were prepared to work very hard for a short spell to get some quick money. The stable working population of Cartwrights had worked itself into the rhythm of the firm's trade cycle, and tolerated this spurt before the summer holidays. But to the workmen who were only passing through, work at Cartwrights was unattractive: 'You get one or two, who've never been to any other "shop" and don't know what it's like outside, the old 'uns, but there's only a few.' There was a hint that in the valley a fairly large shifting population of workmen was looking for a good place of work to settle into. Cartwrights was not such a place—'T'best places y'have to wait till somebody dies to get a job there'.

Management

This was a large mill, and its owner was not the awesome figure that Stoner Cartwright had been—he appeared once during the time of the study, looking in for five minutes with a party of visitors. Nor were any of the other directors much in evidence. Once a day a man in a white coat strode round, his brows knit in thought, but he never spoke and men certainly never approached him, 'You musn't let him see owt, you know.' The immediate figure of authority was James Shaw, who did not apply any known policy. Cartwrights seemed like a machine which, once started, would run by itself without any guidance. Beyond James Shaw was not a commanding group, 'them', so much as an indifferent 'nobody'.

The Factory Act poster in a passageway was ignored, and conditions of heat and humidity were bad. Yet men didn't even bother to ask if they could have the fans on, or the windows open. If you did, 'nobody took any notice'. There was much satisfied comment when a factory inspector arrived and made James Shaw have all the windows opened and the fans switched on. 'Aye, it's about time an' all.' This was not so much an expression of corporate hostility and truculence towards a management, as a feeling that it seemed to be nobody's responsibility to see to these working conditions. In case of accidents, a woman weaver could treat minor cuts, but, 'We're lucky to have a pair of scissors'. In spite of frequent warnings, a hole in the shed floor was left untouched until an accident happened.

This dislocation between workpeople and managers was aggravated by lack of organisation in the finishing shed. Overtime was compulsory, which meant that there was so much work to be done that the firm offered a high wage and stated the hours to be worked, and any workman who wanted shorter hours could go elsewhere. At times this involved a six-day week, with hours from 7.15 a.m. to 6 p.m.; a sixty-hour week was common. There was no point in asking for time off, so when a man felt that he had worked enough overtime he would take a day or two off, secure in the knowledge that someone could always be found to do his job. Perhaps a minimal organisation had once been attempted, and here and there were men who could regard themselves as being employed for one job only. Many of these jobs could be picked up in a few hours, since their main requirement was physical effort without much dexterity. As a further disturbance, the flow of work switched unpredictably from process to process as each large order went through in a batch, so that men had to be taken off one machine and put on another with a different partner as often as twice a week. Men said that this 'mugging about' was worse during the winter months when there was scarcely work enough to give them all the basic forty-five-hour week.

All this contributed to men's feeling of anonymity. And further confirmation was the knowledge that only if you had spent *fifty* years working for this firm would you receive the firm's pension of £1 a week. 'There was an old man a bit since that got a bit slow, and t'head-ender must have complained. They found him another job, but he said he couldn't do that, so that were it. He'd finished.'

At one time none of the work was done on piece-rates. When this system had first been introduced there was no satisfactory way of checking the amount of work that a man had actually done. One of the machines brushed the cloth, and each piece had to be brushed several times, depending on the finish required. It took a very keen eye to detect that a piece had only been brushed twice instead of three times. And it would also have involved a huge amount of clerical work to check that all the identification numbers, which were entered as pieces of cloth passed through the machine, were those of actual pieces and not numbers made up by the workman on the machine.

Almost three years before, the whole system had been tightened up. A series of ingenious clocks and checks narrowed the margin of doubt on each job, and many other processes were timed for piece-rate working in an attempt to speed up the whole department. All rates were fixed by the management, without any reference to the men doing the jobs—there was no question of negotiation. Rates were fixed with an eye to the market in labour, against competition from other firms. Cartwrights was no different from other firms in the valley in this. 'It's all piece-rates. They'll vary a bit in different places, but they can't vary much, and you'll find people leaving and going to other places and then they come back a bit later and say that they aren't doing any better.'

Satisfactions

Management was based quite simply on money without paternalism. No attempt was made to fix a man's allegiance to the firm, or to consult his opinions and needs in any respect. What satisfaction did men find working under these conditions?

There was less sense of anonymity among the older men who had worked at Cartwrights all their lives. They still felt pride in Cartwrights' world record, and excused the changes which had taken place in the firm on the grounds that, 'You can't run a big place like you could a small place, and trade's changing.' Younger men prepared to leave as soon as they got the chance; such tolerance to them was simply a lack of ambition. The men who stayed at Cartwrights were on 'nice, steady jobs', where work was skilled and the pace careful. This skilled work offered a certain pride in workmanship which was denied most men in the finishing shed. Perching was a skilled job which commanded the respect of other workers. Cutting, too, was rated a skilled job, although one old man regretted that this was more tradition than reality: 'Ah think it dates from t'times when they used to cut t'cloth laid out on a table wi' shears by hand. It were t'most skilled job there were then, but I hardly think it's skilled now we've got these machines.'

Even the other men on the routine jobs could still shrewdly judge the workmanship of different types of cloth going through the mill. They *felt* which cloth was good, which bad. They had learned to detect differences in texture by a quick rub with hard finger-tips, and even when there was no need to touch a piece, men tended to reach out and pat or stroke the piled cloth, or run their hands over cloth revolving on rollers for the satisfying feel of it. But soon, as trade changed, even this would be impossible:

'They used to make a lot of good quality worsted. There were none o'this stuff then. D'you know what this stuff's made of? Old socks! Old socks with a bit o'good stuff in to hold it together. There's a lot of synthetics in now, that fibre they make out o'wood. They put owt in; rats' tails and seals' tails all mixed in among.'

Work was so arranged that conscientiousness was penalised by loss of wages. The piece-rate system operated against the skilled workman, who must go slowly and carefully on difficult work, and in favour of the unskilled men who did easy work at a fast rate. There was no other judgment than speed of working. So, when a young workman fetched the foreman to look at an unsatisfactory piece, 'He said it wasn't one of his. That's what irritates me about this place; everybody says it's not their fault. Look at that piece. We'll put it through now, instead of stopping it here, and it'll go right up to t'warehouse and they'll have to send it back from there.' All the time this was happening the young man was losing time and money. On the next machine where they were 'wetting out' cloth, there was actually a fight between two men, one of whom was trying scrupulously to examine the work and send back faulty pieces. The stronger man wouldn't have this, because too much time was lost. 'Time's money these days. You can't *afford* to help other people else you're losing money yourself.'

Fiddling

Because the wages had been calculated as the minimum which the firm could pay and still attract 'labour', men felt that they were entitled to earn the piece-rate bonus on each job. But they were up against a difficulty here. Unless they worked ceaselessly, with no breaks, or even breakdowns, they could not earn this maximum bonus. The pace of work was uncomfortably fast and they felt the need of a break, which was in any case a social occasion necessary to the life of the mill. Both the 'head-ender' and the 'tail-ender' went for these breaks at the same time so the machine had to be stopped. It was impossible to assess the objective truth of men's statements that the time-rates were unattainable; perhaps the small breaks and the inevitable delays in finding work among the heaps of cloth on the scrays would have added up to meet the discrepancies. Everyone was quite convinced that the rates were at fault. Depending on the particular process the complaint was different: some machines had clocks which 'wouldn't do the units' (i.e. even if they ran all the time the revolution counter would never register the firm's estimate of revolutions per hour on which the pay scale was based); 'Look at that. That's t'fastest cutting machine there is and he's speeding that up even. When

Ah tell other folk at other places how much I have to do here they won't believe it.' Men felt that they could not honestly earn the wage which was their due.

Some of their resentment at this situation was visited upon the manager who had timed the machines and fixed the rates. The stories told about this man varied with the teller. Nobody knew what had become of him, but all agreed that he left under suspicious circumstances: he had been fired for inefficiency, they said, because he got no orders for the mill.

Yet in spite of the alleged slowness of the machines, or excessively fast rates, everyone always earned the maximum bonus. To achieve this, men 'fiddled' the amount of work entered on their time sheets until it agreed with the rate for the job. 'Fiddling' took various forms, depending on the work process. It was always dishonest from the management's point of view, but it did not mean inferior workmanship. Cutters explained their system; 'Nobody can tell, you see, how many cuts it's going to take' (how many times a piece must go through the machine). 'Well, what we do here, say we've got a piece to cut we give it one cut and we put down two.' Another job allowed a man to perform two paid processes at once. When all else failed men could look back through their work-books and select one or two serial numbers of pieces which had been done a few days before. The understanding with the management was: 'They know we fiddle. James Shaw said to me the other day, 'Fetch your wage book, your fiddle book.' *They* fiddle. They fiddle the factory inspector; they tell him there's no children of fifteen working overtime.' If men were caught 'fiddling' they knew they would be sacked, unless the firm was very short of labour, in which case they were merely suspended. Under these circumstances there could be no question of 'rights', 'duties', or obligations in work. 'T'management won't listen to you. It's all Cartwrights' way here, so if you can fiddle a bit you do. It pays you to.'

Men's discomfort in these conditions was expressed, characteristically, in the jokes which covered over uneasiness, and which might eventually hint at an incipient insensitivity to the finer issues involved. 'The men aren't greedy here. They just want a fucking lot.' Two men who were still working when the buzzer went for dinner were jeered, 'All for ruddy fourpence.' The ware-house where piece-rates were tighter was known as 'the White City'. At heart they seemed sickened at the rush for money: 'It's not so bad now when there's a lot of work, but when there isn't so much they'll be fighting each other for it. You'll see a piece on a cart and there'll be a mad rush of ten bodies after it.' They felt, without ever quite expressing directly, that breakdown of social sanctions which came from the absence of a stable com-munity in the mill and their lack of any voice with the manage-ment. In some respects they had preferred the days when Stoner Cartwright would sack a couple of managers, for in place of these managers who were part of a community in the valley had come distant figures, 'foreigners' or bankers. The new man offered money, but little else; what the workmen wanted was a sense of 'belonging' to society. Behind much of their discontent was a call for a corporate voice such as the unions had once possessed. But there was no such union at Cartwrights, nor could there ever be without a supporting community. Men's response under these circumstances was not to organise but to leave and look for a 'better shop'.

Laziness

This is a leaflet about 'work' entitled Laziness, handed out to boys at a Huddersfield secondary modern school in Morning Assembly.

What is your ambition and how are you shaping towards it? Do you welcome the tough spots in life because they test you and develop your character or do you always dodge difficulties and take the easy way? Remember that backbones achieve more than wish-bones.

Laziness makes all things difficult but industry makes all easy; and he that riseth late must trot all day and shall scarce overtake his business at night: while laziness travels so slowly that poverty soon overtakes him.

So said Benjamin Franklin, American statesman and scientist, the inventor of the lightning conductor.

One of the aims of our school is to help us to have *the right attitude to work* at all times not simply when it is interesting but also when it is hard and tedious; no work is interesting and new all the time. We should remember that employment is not provided just so that we can earn money. Naturally we need money in order to live, but another important purpose of work is *to produce something or to serve other people*.

If you are lazy you will not like this. It will make you feel uncomfortable.

Christian Code for the Young Employee:

(1) I believe in team work with my fellow workers.
(2) I will respect the firm's property.
(3) I believe there should be no ragging or larking at work: it is dangerous and hinders production.
(4) I must be honest.
(5) I must learn persistently and patiently.
(6) I know that obedience and courtesy are signs of strength and not weakness.
(7) I believe in good timekeeping and attendance.
    Lewis Carroll wrote these words:

> Man naturally loves delay
> And to procrastinate
> Business put off from day to day
> Is always done too late.
>
> Better to be before your time
> Than e'er to be behind
> To ope the door, while strikes the clock
> *That* shows a punctual mind.

Hymn 69. ('Fight the good fight . . .')

We will close the service with the School Prayer remembering that happiness comes to those who earnestly work.

Chapter Six

ON THE BOWLING
GREEN

'Huddersfield is the stronghold of Yorkshire bowls,' said the President. He was shovelling coal from the railway sidings into his wagon. He ran a one-man business, and at work wore an old sack round his waist like an apron, a dusty felt hat, a dirty grey shirt with a silk tie pulled so tight that the knot was minute. His coal-streaked suit had leather shoulder pads fitted into it. Probably ten years before he would have been formally dressed in these same clothes—suit, hat, silk tie—for a presentation ceremony on the green. At work his talk ran mostly on gambling and bowls —sometimes veering out of Yorkshire into little patches of middle class 'one does this, one does that'.

'We've had to alter a clause in our rules to say that you could have money prizes. But that was to remove abuses that were creeping in. These competitions, like the *News of the World*, they gave them vouchers. But the chap who was bowling, he'd be able to take this voucher to the shop and say 'how much cash will you give me for it?' We're really amateurs here—over in Lancashire it's more of a professional game. They're betting mad—they bowl all the year round, sweep the snow off greens. They go for the bookies, you see, and you get a different sort of people going. But as far as we're concerned, the bookies aren't there. Once you get that element creeping in, you get nasty stories about bowlers not bowling their best. We've never had one proved, but we've suspected one or two. People nowadays are betting mad. They're not content with the wage they get, are they? I reckon the ordinary man earns a good wage nowadays, but they don't seem content with it; there's pools and there's Bingo. And these 'ere One Armed Bandits, well it's absolute foolishness is that. I've sat back and I've studied, now what makes a young fellow put sixpence in that thing—and being in business myself you know,

I sometimes see my money going in as well. If you understand what I mean? Money that should have been paid to me. You have to keep quiet though about it.'

The bowls played in Huddersfield is Crown Green bowls, not the Flat Green bowls played in the Midlands and South. In Crown Green, not only are the woods (bowls) biased, but the green slopes away in every direction from the crown (centre). So in trying to get the woods nearer the jack than your opponent can, you must match bias against bias. I don't know where Crown Bowls originates from, and have not been able to find out. The Flat Green bowls of the south is really the old aristocratic game of bowls—Drake on Plymouth Hoe—and is very much, with its white suits and straw boaters, a middle-class occupation, though of course played by many working-class men. In the past, an Act forbade the people to play bowls, which was the sport of the gentry alone.

Perhaps Crown Bowls is the answer, at least of the industrial classes of the North. Little is known about the other game, Flat Green, in Huddersfield. 'No, I don't know anything about Flat Greens,' said the President. 'I've never been to a game in my life. Of course, there's a lot more skill, you know, in Crown Greens, a lot more skill.'

Huddersfield has thirty-three main bowling clubs, and many more ephemeral ones. The strongest ones are usually bowling clubs, whose whole *raison d'être* is built round the green. Next come the working men's clubs which have a green attached, then Liberal or Conservative clubs with greens, and weakest of all the clubs that spring from factories and mills, or which have tried to build themselves up in a public park. In a good summer there must be 5,000 fairly regular bowlers in Huddersfield. No other sport begins to rival it in numbers of players. In the big events Huddersfield probably enters more players than any other town. The *News of the World* Handicap will attract 350 very skilled bowlers from Huddersfield—half the total entry. The *Yorkshire Merit* will get 400 or so, a quarter of the entry. And there is a whole range of local competitions—knockout, handicap, merit, elimination cup, rose bowl, league. The story is that bowls is an old man's game, and certainly half that 5,000 will be aged fifty or more. But very many younger men are always to be seen on the greens, and there is a permanent scattering of women and teenagers. It would be truer to say that the game *features* old men, puts them conspicuously 'on stage'.

The clubs are very like working men's clubs—a bar, dominoes, whist drives for the Darby and Joan Club on a Monday afternoon, a concert on a Saturday evening, trips away during the summer. But the green makes a difference. It gives an outdoor focus, a stage whose montage demands its special skills and rituals. 'It takes three and a half hours to prepare this green, and during that time we walk seven miles apiece.' There is a vast amount of pegging out, fertilising, worm treading, rolling, airhole making. From time to time, well-paid local experts are called in to bring back the quality of a green. The intensity of concern over the green is far more than that found in local cricket over the maintenance of the pitch. Only at county level does pitch culture equal the felt importance of green culture. 'This green was here twenty-five years before I was born so it'll be a hundred years old anyway. That green over there is older. This is a tricky one, but yon over there is the best one. That old one, we're gonna do it before winter comes, we're gonna get it up to scratch again.'

In the Library

Crown Green bowls is the most popular sport in Huddersfield. It is almost exclusively working class; it has developed from a sport into one of the interlocking cells of community with a local 'club' life growing out from it; there is a certain perplexing intensity when people discuss it, and somehow it has a special importance to the old. The next step was to call in the public library and see what books there were on bowls.

There was one, *Crown Bowls* by E. A. Lundy. The author seemed to be a journalist, or at least a bowling correspondent. He writes about bowls in exactly the same tone and rhetoric that is still found in the literature of working men's clubs and brass bands.

'Bowls is a science, the study of a lifetime, in which you may exhaust yourself but not your subject. It is a contest, a duel, calling for courage, skill, strategy and self-control. It is a test of temper, a trial of honour, a revealer of character. It affords a chance to play the man and act the gentleman. It is a cure for care, an antidote for worry. It also includes companionship with friends, social inter-course, and opportunities for courtesy, kindliness and generosity to an opponent. It provides not only physical health but moral force.'

The author speaks of the 'character building' qualities of bowls, and claims—no doubt justly—that they are quite as strong as the 'character building qualities of cricket'. He laments that there are no school bowling greens, and that such a thing is regarded as unthinkable, incomprehensible by education officials and teachers. He fears that Flat Green bowls with its social prestige and international outlook may spread to the industrial north and destroy the native and more highly skilled game.

He writes most warmly about the two major tournaments in bowling—both of which have taken place since the 1870s in Blackpool. The *Talbot* is the classical pub tournament, but the *Waterloo* is almost as famous. They stand to bowls as Belle Vue does to brass bands. 'As at all historic places, and the *Talbot* is one, an indefinable atmosphere prevails . . . except for visiting the Tower of London nothing has ever impressed me quite as much as my first visit to the *Talbot*.' The field of reference indicates how little of this part of working-class life has come into the 'public' expression of print, yet how very much it is felt as being *there*.

This is the only book on bowls that Huddersfield possessed. It had plenty of books on Flat Green bowls of course—pictures of Drake, W. G. Grace, O.B.E.s, J.P.s, blazers, club ties, panama hats. Huddersfield has no Flat Green bowling, but all the books which have illustrations or hints on technique are frequently taken out. Either the library authorities don't know about Huddersfield, or the Huddersfield working class does not know how to make a library serve them—if it can. For libraries can only concern themselves with those parts of social life that have entered the 'public' realm of books. Here, casually discovered, was the old, invisible frontier between the classes.

Finals of the Oldfield Cup

On an evening early in September, the semi-final was being played off in a municipal park by two pairs of young men. One of them had won the rose bowl on the previous Saturday. Standing up outside the bowling hut were thirty or forty keen bowlers, mostly men in their late forties or fifties or early sixties. Round the green, and in other parts, were older men, some of them about seventy, but also a sprinkling of teenagers, strongly supporting the young people on the green. There were not many women: some were relatives of the players, others were the wives of the old men sitting round the green. The group of bowlers round the club-house was very solid and intimate. Everybody knew everybody else; they all talked all the time, making comments on the play, deciding where the players were going to go next, whether they should go into the corner, whether this particular wood was going to 'miss all', or 'run out', 'peg out', or 'narrow'. Quite often they were wrong. In fact it seemed as though fifty per cent of the time they were wrong and that the average person making wild guesses could have guessed as well. Bowling always provided an erratic sort of comment and no one could be wrong all the time; there was no stigma in being wrong, and quite a satisfaction in being right. One old man was especially prominent at the front of the group, making dogmatic statements about where they ought to go and where they ought not to go. 'Where do you think they'll go next?' argumentatively. 'Nay, they never will. They'll go in yon corner.'

It was getting late by the time this semi-final had finished. It was a very good game, all the players commented on it. When it had finished it was about quarter to eight, dusk was beginning to fall and two older men stepped on to the green to play the winners. They were dressed quite differently. One of the younger men was wearing a flowery American-type shirt outside his trousers. The other was wearing white shirt and dark-grey trousers, with suede shoes. Of the two older men one was wearing baggy brown trousers, half a suit, with a pullover. The other man was wearing an unbuttoned waistcoat, cloth cap and baggy dark-blue trousers. He had a slight limp. As they played the two older men took charge of the game and ran up a fair lead before the young ones found their feet again. It got darker and darker and people began to complain, 'It's not fair, I shouldn't like to be out there. There's people round here criticising, and I shouldn't like to be out there and be criticised in the darkness, you can't see where you're going. They ought to stop it, play tomorrow. They could play tomorrow. It's committee's fault for having them play so late.' The Secretary prowled up and down the back looking savage, 'I called a meeting last Saturday for grumblers, but none of them turned up, but there's plenty here tonight.' He changed his tune eventually and became rather apologetic as it got very dark. In the end he apologised for the inconvenience, but as it turned out everyone now began to enjoy it. People began to make jokes about floodlights, 'Are you going to turn the lights on them, Mr. Heap, or perhaps Mrs. Heap would like to do it?' 'You can't turn these thousand-watt lamps on yet, not for another ten minutes, you'll be wasting electric.' 'There it is' as the street lamps came on. 'Can you see yon floodlight just starting up? They've fixed it a bit low though, haven't they?' And so on. As it got still darker the umpire put his handkerchief on top of the jack so that the player could see it. The old man from Turnbridge was indignant, 'That's not allowed. You can hold it behind the jack but not put it on top.' Much argument over the niceties of the point of illuminating the jack. There were arguments over precedents: 'They ought never to play this, in this light.' 'What do you mean, ought never to play? We've played games on this green, finals, when they've had to strike matches in t'corner to find where t'jack was.' 'What about Linthwaite Hall last week? They played t'finals and they played later than this.' 'Aye, but Linthwaite Hall isn't here, it isn't *this* part.' But such argument was submerged in the excitement of running from one corner of the green to the other. It got darker and darker so that the spectators could hardly see the woods. They began to step over the edge of the green. It was a very tight finish at twenty all. The crowd made joking comments to the man who looked after the bowls hut. 'You'll be dry, won't you, John?' A Corporation employee, he was waiting to close up. Eventually he switched the lights off, and the prizes were presented in total darkness.

The Champion of Champions

The last month of the season is a long line of finals, climax after climax. The days darken more quickly and the brilliant, succulent green under the rolling black 'woods' begins ever to little, to fray. Each evening is more tense than the last; arguments about minute points of precedent, lore, and personality, crop up all the time. And always there is the race to reach the climax before the darkness falls.

On the last day of the formal season, came the Champion of Champions Merit. The park greens were already closed, some keen bowling clubs would play for another week or two yet, but the Champion of Champions meant the end of the game till next spring.

It was a competition between some of the winners of the better known Merit Matches in Yorkshire. There was the Working Men's Club Merit winner, the Murrfield Merit winner, the Yorkshire Merit winner, Conservative League winner and so on. Some sixteen players in all. The prize was not large, something like £20 for the winner. The chief attraction was the honour of winning the final merit.

The bowling club at Springwood was very ramshackle: two huts, in the smaller of which tea was served. Besides this, there was the large club room itself, where beer was being pulled. Entrance was two shillings. At about half past three there was a large crowd spreading round half the bowling green. Benches were arranged over this distance, and these were necessary, because most of the spectators were over the age of fifty. Quite a few of them old age pensioners. There were few younger men aged forty and below. There were few women, perhaps one to every ten men. Most of the spectators congregated on the flight of steps leading out of the club room. But by the time the players were down to the quarter finals, the spectators were grouped four deep and thicker along the club side of the green. In among the spectators were the bookmakers. There were four of these, two of them more enthusiastic than others. One man stood on a chair, another just stood quietly in the corner. As each game proceeded, they would shout to the scorers, 'What's t'game now?' And on receiving the score would rapidly work out the odds for that game. All the betting was on the final, and as the afternoon progressed the ground became littered with torn up betting slips as the various favourites went out. Much the most conspicuous bookmaker was a fat man wearing enormous pin-stripe trousers, fancy waistcoat, dark coat, and a bowler hat. He had great features, red face, glary eyes. He was a familiar figure, many of the crowd talked and joked with him throughout the afternoon. He had men about him whom he called his 'slaves'. They were also conspicuously dressed. One of them, Jim, was wearing a black Homburg, and a black coat like his boss. The other looked more American, a sharp-faced man, less conspicuously dressed in light grey suit, and trilby. His job was to stand behind the other book-makers as they were making their book, and if possible see how they were going on. He signalled their bets to his master by the usual tick tack code. Betting was very complicated. The odds changed with every wood at some stages. Thus in five minutes in the semi-final the odds dropped from five to one, down to three to one and then to five to two. Nearly everybody seemed to make a bet at some stage or other. Many of them by astute betting managed to back both players in the finals at reasonable odds, so that they couldn't lose by the end of the afternoon. Bets were quite large, usually in paper money, a pound or two. The book-makers themselves became interested in the game as the afternoon progressed and began to shout encouragement. The game went on amid much noise. As each round was played, one match in particular would attract the crowd's fancy, perhaps the most important game, or the one with the closest odds. It was noticeable how bad some of the ends were. This green was unfamiliar to most of the players, only two of whom were local players. Every green had its own idiosyncrasies and this one had many, so that quite often in the early stages of the game, ends would be widely scattered and local players would be able to say that they could bowl a better end. 'I could do better than that. That's club bowling, it isn't merit bowling, they haven't *bowled* this after-noon.' Again it was striking how much material for speculation each end provided. As soon as a wood started its course the cries went up, 'He's none up', or 'He's short', and as each assertion was made other people loudly disagreed. And with comments like these, there would be partisan cries of 'Miss all' or 'Run out' as the spectators encouraged their own particular player and dis-couraged his opponent. They shouted advice to the players, 'Strike!', 'Get some bowling done'.

In the manual of bowls the players were recommended to learn how to strike, and to practise this, that is, to deliberately knock their opponent's wood away from the jack with their own. But some of the crowd considered that striking was unfair, or 'lucky'. It was unsporting compared with the player who tried to win only by 'bowling'. One of the players in particular employed the strike to good effect and tempers became frayed in the crowd.

The players were of widely different ages. The oldest player was seventy-six, a man called Jagger. He was not much more than five feet two high, wearing flat cap, serge pin-stripe suit, and black boots. His appearance caused much satisfied comment, 'Where are these young bowlers now, that's showing 'em up a bit, i'nt it.' Earlier in the season, at the Yorkshire Merit, people said he couldn't last out through the hot day's play, but he'd won. Now that the weather was colder, people said he wouldn't last through a cold day, and towards the evening there was much comment when Jagger was seen to be putting his coat on. Others of the players were about thirty years old. Jagger was an unspectacular player, very dour, winning the crowd's approval for his unshakability.

Each of the players tended to exhibit his personality to the crowd. A younger player for instance was 'A cocky little bugger', because he carried himself very confidently and he was given to signalling points before the final wood had come to rest, or to making confident statements about who was 'on' from a good distance. If his opponent had some luck, or even if he hadn't, he would sometimes shake his head ruefully and talk to the crowd. Or hold out his hands in despair. The crowd were half inclined to like this, but in the end they preferred the more staid play of Jagger.

The players were very active, some of the older men in particular running across the green to look at ends and then coming back before they bowled their next wood. As each round ended there was a flow into the club house to get more beer, a short intermission for drinking and then when the next round started, a flow out onto the steps again.

The Merit lasted from two o'clock in the afternoon until seven in the evening, going on into the dusk. As the game approached the finals the bookmakers offered shorter and shorter odds, until finally hardly anyone was prepared to take them. Now and again they would resort to phoney betting with each other. One bookmaker would call out the odds, the other one would offer to take him. But no money ever exchanged hands between them. The 'slaves' put money on with their boss, and ostentatiously passed pound notes across. But the crowd grew wise to this one as well. There was much dissatisfaction with the standard of bowling. One man shouted out, 'There's one bowler that would have licked them all.' And gave the name of a well-known player of a few years ago. There were mutters of approval from the back. Finally at the beginning of the final between two old age-pensioners, one man, aged sixty-five, the other man Jagger aged seventy-six, the betting ceased. Jagger won the match easily. Champion of Champions. Great applause, a presentation in the gathering dusk. Then most of the people strolled home, but a few stayed to drink in the club house. There was no check on members drinking, and no fear of the police coming. It felt like the end of a long, half-understood ceremony. The players and spectators sipping a final pint, or sensing the autumn nip as they made their way home to fireside and television. All tension had gone.

What is Bowls About?

I don't know. There is a kind of passion about the activity that I've never understood, and which seems different from many other sporting interests. But there are three headings under which the question can be met, though whether they penetrate is doubtful.

First, bowls belong to the same plane of community as working men's clubs. In a club, the focus is the beer, and whereas the tendency in a pub (though often defeated) is to treat the establishment as a shop that sells beer, in a club the activities spread out star-wise. 'Regulars' are replaced by members; long hours go into playing dominoes or reading papers and spending nothing; there are concerts, trips, treats, that bring in children, wives, the old; there are cells of special activities—band practice, snooker team, union meetings. Bowling clubs are very similar to all this; they too are a society of members, chiefly men, who link up with other groupings—part of the network of community. But with them, the green has more importance than the bar. An interesting example is what happens when a working-class group sets up a bowls club in a municipal park. There are always difficulties between the club and the committee of the local council or its officer. The source is often the same: the officials, and the middle class councillors see the park as a public amenity. They don't much like the idea of clubs since this suggests closed membership, and they want to run the green as an object in itself. If you want to play bowls, here it is, if you don't then go somewhere else and do something else. It is a single commodity like beer in the public house. What the working-class want, and try to make of it, is rather different. They want to build around the green the familiar, interlocking cells of community. The official who turned out the lights on the presentation ceremony was implying, brusquely, that he didn't like the unfamiliar and inconvenient activities that grew up around a plain municipal bowling green. But usually this working-class world was lost in darkness, not through anyone's hostility but through their ignorance. As the library indicated, middle class Huddersfield—especially the educated mobile middle class—hardly knew that substantial working-class interests existed.

Second, bowls is a sporting expression of the northern working class similar to other examples. As with Rugby League (which was formed in the George Hotel, Huddersfield) there is the awareness of a middle class or south-country sport which is not quite what they want. Rugby Union or Flat Green bowls are discussed in much the same way. Both are regarded as snooty (though working men may play bowls in the South and Welsh rugby is certainly known to be different). Both are considered to be less skilled. The northern games, adapted to working-class life, allow a mild professionalism—a matter of earning a few pounds on the side. Both allow a bit of gambling, yet at the same time, besides the drink and gambling moments, both have their moral, Methodist tone. And both are very concerned with the spectator. This doesn't make them passive rather than active sports as is sometimes argued about other games—rather they are individual or team activities within a strong communal setting. The spectator is important.

And as with Rugby League and brass bands there is a missionary feeling about the 'movement'. Rugby League is clearest here, with its annual, hopeless trip to Wembley. Brass bands travelling by coach to the Albert Hall are similar. There is no traditional missionary journey of like stature in bowls. But nearer home the spirit of pilgrimage and festival is quite as strong. With Rugby League there is a feeling that Odsal stadium, Bradford, is a very special amphitheatre, different from other grounds. With brass bands, Belle Vue, Manchester, has this place. With bowls, it's the *Talbot* and the *Waterloo* at Blackpool. One can't, I think, trace an older folk festival which in transmuted form now expressed itself in the Belle Vue competition or the *Talbot* tournament. But in spirit and function, they are not so dissimilar. Perhaps this is one subsidiary reason why they don't find their way so readily into the normal 'public' literature and why they don't make sense—and so difficulties arise—when approached by middle class officials as if they were middle class activities. They are certainly a quite different 'folk' expression from the occasional flurries of school maypole dancing or Rotary Club morris men that one sometimes encounters in Huddersfield or Halifax; and very much more powerful.

Third, just as football—Huddersfield Town versus Leeds United —offers something like tribal conflict, with its strongest appeal to and involvement with the young and middle-aged men, so bowls is peculiarly potent for the old. Young men play it, and play it successfully. Yet they're treated as exceptions even when they are not. The meaning of bowls lies largely in its service to the old. On the green, the old men can look as vigorous as the young— it's noticeable how much they run and jump as soon as they are 'on stage'. The smooth rolling 'woods' don't require a young man's strength, and possibly there are some virtues—crossing bias with bias, knowing a green's peculiarities—that age is more likely to have. I rather doubt this though, and suspect that the premium placed on long experience is much exaggerated—another part of the old man 'myth'. The green, itself so aggressively young and fresh to look at and yet paradoxically so old and cherished, is a very special setting where an old man can, for a brief spell, be young again. Fringed by the perpetually arguing crowd, shadowed by the coming dusk, the old men briskly pursue the smooth-running woods over the green grass. One begins to see why the genuine strength demanded by 'striking' should be doubtful play, and to half-comprehend how these obscured patterns of living command such loyalties—and make good sense.

Chapter Seven

RIOT

Like most trouble, it began on Saturday night. It was 10.30 and in the town centre bars and cinemas emptied and trolley-bus queues lengthened. Venn Street, with a cinema at one end, a dance hall at the other, and pubs in between, was—for fifteen minutes—as busy with departing crowds as during the mid day shopping rush.

A motorist climbed into his car, and revved up hastily. Within ten yards he collided with a youth who had walked off the pavement. Within ten seconds, half-a-dozen sixteen-year-old boys were banging on his windows and pulling the doors open. 'You knocked our mate down. We'll get you.' People stopped to watch. Moments later the car was surrounded by forty people.

Farther along, a man had collapsed. Two policemen were putting him in an ambulance. They left him, marched briskly along Venn Street, collared the noisiest boy and dragged him away into Kirkgate. As they got out of Venn Street the boy swung round and butted a policeman in the jaw. P.C. Hilton couldn't eat a meal for three days. The policeman struck back, and at this, the other lads, following at a distance, rushed into the mêlée. The cinemas spilled out more and now Venn Street and Kirkgate were filled with a noisy crowd, already 500 strong and rapidly rising. Policemen arrived hurriedly in twos and threes. The crowd jeered them. As they tried to break it up, incidents broke out all along the street. P.C. Bottomley tried to 'move on' a 23-year-old engineer. 'You can't stop me, copper. You're all the same, you coppers. Let's see what you can do.' He was arrested. Outside 'The Fleece', P.C. Mayhew moved on another group. An apprentice bricklayer rallied them, yelling 'Push off, copper. We're doing nowt wrong.' More police moved in, more arrests were made. Police cars arrived, and almost immediately were met by bricks

and stones. People were cut and bruised as random and richo-
cheting missiles flew from both pavements. Police bundled two
prisoners into a van, and a young butcher dragged its door open
again: 'Come on lads, get out of it.' There was a fight around the
van, and as more police hustled in, the prisoners were held and
the rescuers bundled after them. Another policeman brought a
new prisoner to the vans, and a trainee miner broke out of the
crowd, knocked his helmet off and closed in, only to be trapped
by fresh policemen backing up.

The crowd was now probably 1,000 strong and almost every
available policeman in Huddersfield was in Venn Street. Rapidly
and efficiently they broke the crowd down, scattered it, drove it
towards the bus stops. The brick-throwing slackened. No one
was caught. The crowd dispersed very reluctantly, leaving odd
pockets to make defiant stands. P.C. Keen cleared the pavement
in front of the 'Palace', and moved up Kirkgate where a few
youths leaned stubbornly against the walls. A foot pushed out,
tripped him, there was a shout of 'get that copper', but almost at
once the attacker ran. Police gave chase, and ran him down.
Sporadically, reluctantly, the riot ended.

What was the Riot About?

On Monday ten youths, mostly apprentices in their late teens,
were sentenced in court. The Chief Constable of Huddersfield
made a careful speech. It was not a race riot in any way, he said.
Nor was it a drunken brawl. Nobody arrested 'was in any way
under the influence'. 'I cannot give you a reason for it. People
went simply mad.'

Others felt they could give reasons. The Rev. Frank Thewlis
feared this might be the beginnings of race war. 'I would make an
appeal from the pulpit—but what's the use? It would fall on
wrong ears.' A Labour councillor who was also a newspaper
reporter felt 'that this is only the start of a massive wave of
violence in the town. Huddersfield could be the centre of open
warfare between white and coloured people'.

The next day the Huddersfield Free Church council put it into a
different context. Their President now saw it as part of the old
battle in the working class—the drinkers versus the dry. 'Tem-

perance organisations have a different problem today, not absolute drunkenness, but those who get a few drinks inside them and are more liable to run into trouble.'

One day later, the editorial in the *Yorkshire Post* considered it from a further angle, and suggested that fear of the Bomb was the root trouble. 'Its immediate offshoot in Britain might be to make people want to cling together, to move about the open in crowds. From this springs a hatred of authority, of the "Establishment" as the main culprit (*"They* got us in this mess') and thence an impulse to anarchy.'

The popular press ignored such theories, but splashed the story big under such banners as 'The Night The Town Went Mad'.

The Second Saturday

Following the press publicity, the police took precautions. The next Saturday night they lined Venn Street and Kirkgate with dozens of men, and waited for 10.30. As the cinemas and pubs closed the street rapidly filled with a crowd of more than 500, plus newsmen. Jeering began, and once more the police started to break the crowd up. Two teenage youths began a squabble. P.C. Vickers told them to 'move on'. Girl friends shouted 'We'll go when we want', 'Let's take our time', and the little group retreated into a pub yard where, with the crowd and cameramen around them and police a few yards away, the youths restarted their squabble. P.C. Vickers pushed his way through, the girls told him to 'go to bed'. When they refused to move, he grabbed one and caught her hair. Flash bulbs popped. Boys came to her rescue, and her brother almost had her free before he was overpowered. The girls had to be dragged screaming to the police box in the Market Place. The booing and jeering was deafening. 'Don't be pushed round by the police. They're nothing.' 'Don't be moved by these coppers.'

But the police had stationed their men with care, and again, the crowd was broken up. By midnight, when the last trolleys left, only tiny groups remained here and there.

What had it been about this time? In court on Monday the police said that people simply waited 'to see what was going to happen'. The papers covered both Saturday night trouble and

Monday morning in court. Again they splashed the story—this time with pictures—'GIRLS URGED ON MOB', 'RIOT TOWN STREET BATTLES'.

Who Threw the Orange Peel?

On the following Wednesday evening Huddersfield Town had a match with Leyton Orient. After thirty minutes the Huddersfield centre-half, Bob Parker, playing in his first match, was injured in a tackle and taken to hospital. Shortly afterwards, Leyton scored the opening goal of the match. There was some booing of the Orient players.

Towards the end of half-time as the players were coming back on the field, schoolboys threw pieces of orange peel into the Leyton goalmouth. The referee came across to see what it was. Consequently, the second half began one minute late.

On Thursday morning most of the popular papers picked up the story. 'The hoodlums of riot town Huddersfield, in the news for their Saturday night frolics, were at it again last night.' 'A group of fans pelted Leyton goalkeeper, Frank George, with rubbish.'

That night, the *Huddersfield Examiner* attacked 'those irresponsible youths who take such a strange yet unsporting delight in booing the opposition'. But both the Mayor and the Chief Constable made statements primarily attacking, not the 'youths' but the popular press: 'It's malicious. I think this sort of sensational publicity is wicked.'

Saturday Night Again

On the third Saturday evening, another crowd of 400-500 gathered on the same streets at the same time, again covered by pressmen. The police were ready, and almost immediately split the crowd in two and moved in. There was the same jeering, the same refusal to move on. An apprentice moulder stood his ground and swore back. He was arrested and in the words of the court report 'He had to be assisted into the police van'. Similar incidents followed. There were shouts of 'You can't stop me, copper', 'You're all the same, you coppers', followed by scuffles, jeering, arrests. Afterwards the police claimed that the crowd was stirred up by a 19-year-old asphalter whom they arrested—'as a direct result of his behaviour, the crowd became increasingly hostile to the police'. The asphalter claimed he had just got off a trolley bus and was walking down to the Beast Market for some fish and chips. He saw the crowds, and waved to a friend. The next thing he knew, he was being rushed into a police van. 'It's a bit of a liberty if you can't go down to the fish shop on a Saturday night.' He was sentenced to three months.

The Last Saturday

Everyone waited for the next episode. On the fourth Saturday another crowd—riddled with pressmen—tried to gather at the ritual hour. But the police were again masters of the scene. In full strength and perfectly posted, they broke up the crowd before it could establish an identity. Incidents were nipped in the bud, and by 11.45 most survivors were in the last bus queues, and Venn Street belonged to policemen alone. In the No. 30 bus for Almondbury, seven youths recognised a young reporter seeing his girl friend home.

'You're a reporter, aren't you?'

'I saw you down in Venn Street, and you put us all in the paper.'

'I'm going to kill you.'

Instead he kicked him, and on the stationary bus the pushing and kicking continued.

'You'll be dead meat when you get off.'

The girl was roughly handled and frightened. The reporter, Paul Morgan, broke free, got off the bus and made off in the direction of Kirkgate to get police help. He picked up a policeman and an inspector and came back to board the bus. There were shouts of 'Morgan has brought the cops, lads', and on the pavement a new fight broke out. One tried to kick the inspector, who dropped his stick and pulled another youth in front of him. This second one caught the kick in his eye and staggered out of the fight. Another picked up the inspector's stick and belaboured him with it, but all were overpowered by more police arriving from Kirkgate. So ended the last of the Huddersfield riots.

Riot

What Caused the Riots?

The riots began accidentally: a hasty motorist, a minor collision, half-a-dozen angry youths, and a cinema crowd. That might have been the end of it. But the latent hostility of the crowd switched quickly from the motorist to the gathering numbers of uniformed policemen. In court, the Chief Constable could not explain the trouble. But, at this stage, it was, fairly evidently, an anti-police riot. The crowd jeered them, stoned them, swore at them, provoked them. Even in the dulled Court reports you can still hear the word 'copper' as an insult, a well-worn challenge, a spit of contempt:

'Push off, copper.'

'You can't stop me, copper.'

'You're all the same, you coppers.'

The energy behind the first riot was the under-surface hatred of the police by the working class. And this is not surprising, nor new. The police are there to serve society as a whole, but very frequently they are the agents of the controlling middle class. Of course this has been dramatically true in past times, and true in more humdrum ways now and in the recent past. I suppose the clearest daily example until five years or so ago were the betting laws which led policemen in plain clothes to sit in pub corners and wait for the coins to appear on the domino table. That particular one has gone, but it's illuminating to look at the police from this angle rather than that of the middle class. The middle class expects help from the police, the working class expects trouble. When a policeman appears on the steps of the Reform Club it is hardly of any consequence to the members; when he appears outside a Huddersfield working men's club the air is tense with protective hostility. The relationship is not nearly so violent as it was, nor as it is now in other societies (the secret police whom the erupting workers hanged in the streets of Budapest in 1956 were themselves members of the working class). But in the milder English way I doubt if the gulf has narrowed as much as it may seem. Police are executants of a law that still remains weighted in favour of the middle classes. Their uniform (how the rioters go for these helmets!) may, to many middle class eyes, be the mark of a servant, as with a hotel commissionaire or a bus conductor. To

116

the working class it announces mastery and threat. In the affluent society the gulfs change their form but remain—policemen now live on small separate housing estates of their own, several degrees superior to council housing. Once they were the tallest and strongest of the workers, uniformed to control the rest. As forms of mastery change, it becomes less and less important that a policeman is tall—inches are gradually knocked off the requirements. But it becomes more and more important that they pass eleven plus or gain G.C.E.s. Every year they move more and more towards the salaried middle class.

Another feature of the earlier Huddersfield riots was that the trouble came almost entirely from apprentices—though they were verbally backed by the older people. Again, the situation is age-old. Working-class hostility always tends to come out first from the apprentices for obvious reasons. And the young miners, butchers and millworkers shouting at the coppers on Saturday night were similar, in many ways, to the 'prentice rioters of Elizabethan London, where they *did* have both a sharp hostility to the ruler's agents and a youth problem (consider their numerical preponderance of the young over the old) that puts ours into perspective.

And yet, though anti-police feeling always runs under the surface and bursts out often enough in Saturday night violence, there is a wall of attitudes and values sealing off the middle class and preventing them from looking at it in this way. When the Chief Constable says: 'People went simply mad'—he is not covering up, he's speaking *his* truth. Perhaps the best example of the wall was the various comments on the riots by the *Huddersfield Examiner*, on this occasion characteristically middle class, in the way it establishes a judgment. After the Leyton Orient incident it was puzzled by 'those irresponsible youths who take such a strange yet unsporting delight in booing the opposition'. Whether the booing is right or wrong ('unsporting') it is hardly 'strange' to a football fan though it may be on the playing fields of the public schools. And the paper certainly saw the police ('Push off, copper') from the other side of the invisible wall.

'They jeered and cat-called at P.C.s and "specials" who took it all in good part and accepted it as something not very far removed from commonplace. More than one officer had a smile on his face as he ushered them away with a gentle but firm "Move along there, please".'

'But the "yobbos"—the lay-abouts and the louts who have nothing better to do in Huddersfield on a Saturday night than start trouble—could get the town a bad name which it does not deserve.'

Examiner, October 2nd.

Curiously, in its account of the attack on the reporter, the *Examiner* whose accounts were otherwise full of 'youths' and 'policemen' referred to him—quite unselfconsciously—as a 'civilian'.

Middle-class Huddersfield simply did not understand what this working-class explosion was about. The Chief Constable ('I cannot give you a reason') and the middle class romance of the *Examiner* are expressions of it.

But the ritual of the Huddersfield riots is interesting too in illustrating the new circlet of non-understanding built around the working-class world. The mass media are, in a sense, more class-less than most British institutions. Certainly they are graded according to the different pockets, ambitions and schooling of different social groups—exactly the same soap is advertised quite differently in *Vogue* and in *TV Times*. But their classlessness is very puzzling. The more 'popular' they are, the more they muffle their presentation of working-class life with a ring of images and attitudes quite as formidable as the old invisible wall. This new barrier is illustrated in the initial process of newspaper thinking as they try to find the 'meaning' of the riots in a familiar news pigeon-hole. The journalist on the Council immediately announces the prospect of race war ('a massive wave of violence', 'open war-fare between white and coloured'). No coloured person was ever involved. The *Yorkshire Post*, from its more philosophical vantage point, explains the challenge to authority as being fear of the Bombs. ('People want to cling together, to move about the open in crowds'.) Then, although the riots don't fit an accepted news slot, they do remain 'new' in an odd way. From the second week onwards, the riots are on a stage, acted before an audience of popping flashbulbs. The presence of newsmen *creates* news. If we read the nonsense that was made out of the orange peel incident, or see the boys and girls almost compelled to scuffling in the pub yard until the policeman reaches for the girl's hair and the cameras flash, then we get a glimpse of the curious relationship between the media and its subject matter—and see why what looks so close (popular reporting with action photographs) is yet quite as distant as the traditional middle class approach voiced by the Chief Constable. And so the riot, begun in that frustration which is part of the common texture of working-class life, ends—meanly, yet symbolically—with the last group of apprentices kicking a reporter and beating a policeman with his own stick of office.

Chapter Eight

JAZZ CLUB

The Jazz Club began in 1952. A group of 16-year-old grammar school boys began to meet in the evenings, blowing trumpets, trombones, clarinets. There was one piano and an uncontrolled number of banjos or basses or washboards. Nobody was leader, and everyone with an instrument could have a go, at once.

There was soon a scattering of girls—14- or 15-year-olds from the lower streams of the girls' grammar school, and the group settled down to regular weekend meetings—and a Thursday rehearsal night—usually in the same hired rooms. It called itself the Jazz Club. There was no particular person in control, no form of membership, no real charge for going there. There was a cash till at the entrance, borrowed from the café downstairs, but no one paid much attention to that. It was friends playing to friends with a competence that increased painfully slowly. But the band became recognisable, and there was no more of the original 'anyone who wants to blow, join us' spirit.

Tony, the trumpeter, arrived on the scene. He'd left grammar school at fifteen and was now an apprentice. Tony became the organiser, a very informal one. He licked the band into better shape, and soon they were picking up the odd pound playing at dances and parties. From time to time, Patrick, the original trumpeter led a breakaway movement and started a rival band in a different place. Players and audience were much the same, but permutations became complex. Breakaways were usually welcomed, as adding more interest to life. They usually led to a change of scene—a room above a new pub, down an unknown side street, or up a rickety fire escape. Breakaways became more common after Patrick started an art course at the technical college. Till then, most of the Jazz Club people had been early leavers from the grammar schools, but Patrick now brought in art and design students and one or two apprentices from the technical college. Most of these too had left grammar school early and then gone to the tech., but quite a few had been at secondary modern schools.

'It might have been a grammar school thing at one time, but I think it's broadening now. But you can't tell at jazz clubs, can you? You can't tell where they come from. They all look the same, and they pretend a bit as well y'know. I know, I've done it myself. I bought a tech. scarf and I thought it was marvellous. My sister's boy friend has a stripey scarf that looks like some university or other. He works in a garage, he's a mechanic—but he's pretending a bit.'

For the next ten years the Jazz Club moved every few months. Sometimes there might be as many as three jazz clubs all playing at once, but it was essentially the same group of people, forming and re-forming. It never organised itself like a working men's club—there was no attempt to get a permanent membership, or to choose people for distinct functions—secretary or treasurer—and no attempt either to get a long lease of any rooms to give the club a more secure physical base. Sometimes a set of rooms was found where 'the crowd' could play at house—cooking lunch, sweeping up, decorating, staying up all night. Fighting or aggressive drunkenness was very rare, love making very private. Intercourse was confined to country walks, or on the couch at the girl's home when her parents had gone to bed. Sexually, 'the crowd' was slightly prudish—swearing for example, was always confined to 'bloody' and 'bugger'. Nevertheless the police were always ready to move the group on. They could usually do this by invoking the fire regulations, and claiming the premises were unsafe. Once a policeman called at 6.30 a.m. and discovered six boys and two girls, all very sleepy—waiting for first bus time so that they could go home and go to bed. It was the fag-end of a jazz-playing, long-talking night. 'He came in and said "What's this? What's going on? We can't have this!" and went to fetch the sergeant. When he came back we'd all gone, except Si. They took Si to the police station and told him "Get out or we'll boot you out".' The next evening there were headlines in the paper 'Six Men and Two Girls Found in Club', and much talk in Huddersfield. But the other-reality of the press picture—as if a Soho enclave of prostitution, drugs, violence had been found in Huddersfield—was such that even 'the crowd's parents didn't connect them with the 'six men and two girls'. 'They were all talking about it at t'mill. My mother asked me if I'd seen it, about where they'd found them girls, and I said "yes". She didn't think I was one of them.'

Only once did the club settle down. This was when one of the band's parents, a bus driver, decided to invest £150 in setting up a club. He would look after the money, his daughter would sell sausages and coffee, his son would lead the band—and, he hoped, he'd see his £150 back many times over. The club was imposed on the crowd, but they didn't mind. There were the usual difficulties of dealing with the police challenge on fire safety, and in getting a music licence. The crowd helped to whitewash the rooms, stuck up classical record covers and travel posters, and painted large, crude murals—like the Penguin photo of D. H. Lawrence carrying away a fainting girl in black. Entry was five shillings. The crowd resented this and most managed to avoid it. The first night they had forty members. The room was bleak and cold. In lines along the roof were coloured lanterns, but more light came from candles in bottles on the tables. The place was vast and could absorb 400. At one end was the band, at the other a row of tea chests with mineral water and coffee for sale on top. The coffee was very bad.

Next week the attendance was up to 100. Again it was bitterly cold, and everyone kept overcoats on. The crowd clustered round tables at one end of the room. The other sixty or so people remained separate—mostly they were 15- or 16-year-old girls from the grammar school. The band complained about their pay. 'He says he'll pay 'em more when he gets on his feet.' Numbers mounted and after a month there were 439 members.

But then Tony, the trumpeter, led a breakaway and opened up in a parish hall. Only twenty of 'the crowd' turned up to his breakaway club and everyone was acutely conscious of the numbers. Judith was in distress, 'Why don't you pack up, there's no point in going on?' A solitary youth came in from the other club, placed his chair in the centre of the empty dancing space, informed them that the other band was 'playing lousy', closed his eyes and listened enthralled. Archie answered Judith: 'Haven't you seen a true artist before?' But the girls were miserable. 'I'm sickened. Help us look for a cellar, that's the only thing that will fetch them back. A cellar with steps to go down and a door with a little spy-hole and a shutter that you can pull back. I know Tony did just the same to Patrick's band, but I'm on their side y'see.'

The bus driver persisted for a year or so, sometimes drawing in several hundred at the weekends and bringing bands from Batley, Wakefield and Leeds. But he couldn't pin 'the crowd' down, his own membership was fickle, the police pressing, and after a while he was glad to get out.

'The crowd' moved from pub to pub, settling longest at a working men's club. Downstairs were the dominoes, drinking, and singing at the working men's club; upstairs in the concert room was the jazz club. It was a cheerless place with a platform at one end and a tiny bar at the other. The usual attendance was around thirty. There was a formal entrance fee, but collection was desultory—everyone claimed exemption. People sat in groups around the tables, drinking slow pints, there was a little jiving— usually the girls partnering each other—and the band went through the formality of announcing each 'number' through the fuzzy microphone. Only two or three people listened with any attention to the music. The musicians didn't listen much either. During a clarinet 'break' the trumpeter would sit back, sip his pint and chat with the trombonist. The bass man would squat on the edge of the platform and talk to a friend drinking at the first table. Everyone took their own solo 'breaks' seriously. Dress was very casual, and the kind of jazz played shifted every few months—from trad to modern and back again, with special 'Brubeck' or 'Armstrong' periods now and again.

Four Members

TONY: Tony the trumpeter came from a railway man's home. His father started the Railway Club in Huddersfield, a working men's club primarily for railway workers.

'My father started it thirty-five years ago. Him and another chap went and borrowed £1,000, no security, from Hammonds—no, not Hammonds—some other brewery, perhaps Bentley and Shaws. I've heard this tale umpteen times. They went up before the directors and they said they wanted to start a club. "Right' how much do you want to borrow?" "Thousand pounds." "What security?" "None."

But they got it. He were secretary then for fifteen years—up till the war.'

Tony went to grammar school, was largely indifferent to it, and left after 'O' level. He took a job in a mill, was apprenticed for seven years, and is now pretty pleased with a £16 a week pay packet. He earns a little out of his playing, and runs an old car. He courted his wife at the club; she was a jazz widow, waiting long hours for him to finish playing. He first heard jazz on the radio, and though he'd had six unhappy years of piano lessons, he took up the trumpet and came along to the Jazz Club a year after it started. He's very sensitive to criticism of his playing and believes that people listen to the music quite carefully.

'I want people to come who understand the music. What gets me is these people who come down on rehearsal night and criticise. They never come at weekends, yet they have the cheek to criticise the music! The number of times when we've just finished and I've heard somebody at the back say "That was a lousy number". Some of 'em'll be feeling the toe of my boot one of these days.'

Tony plays jazz records and reads jazz books—he's full of the New Orleans mythology. He doesn't have any other literary or musical interests, never mentions his work or politics or current affairs. He is much more practical than the other members, and can quite see how money can be made out of jazz when it's needed. He's the one who knows how to get music licences through, how to deal with the fire inspector and the police demands. He's usually the one who finds new rooms for the club. His dress is utterly conventional, and with his moustache, he looks like a flight-lieutenant in civvies. He is completely adjusted to Huddersfield and has none of the anxieties that beset others in 'the crowd'. More than anyone else the Jazz Club crystallises around him, though he's far from being the dominant personality. It's not clear why jazz is so important to him, but except for this private passion, he could well be the secretary of any working men's club in Huddersfield.

PATRICK: Patrick, the rival trumpeter, is a doctor's son, and comes from a quite different social background from anyone else. He and the others are always conscious of it. 'I'm handicapped by my background.' At grammar school he went into the sixth form with the idea of reading science and becoming a doctor too. He had a lot of trouble with mathematics, and there was a conference between parents and teachers, resulting in his changing over to the Arts side: a rare and much-remarked transfer. The idea now was that he would go to university and read law. In the arts sixth he was associated with the small group of working-class boys, often at odds with the school, who formed the original Jazz Club with Patrick as trumpeter.

He lost his position when he left to read Law at London University. This was Tony's opportunity to step in, and the beginning of their ten-year rivalry.

'I'd no idea what Law would be like. You'd think that Law would be a fascinating subject, whereas really it's as dry as dust. You see, I really did work and the family saw me working. But at the end of my first year I passed two papers and failed two. That means I'd got to take the exam again in September, so I worked hard all summer at home. But when I took the exam again I failed *all four* papers. I can't understand it.'

So back to Huddersfield, the Jazz Club and a four-year Art and Design course at the technical college. With jazz and art instead of mathematics and law he soon got over his problems and prepared for a career as a design or colour consultant. Patrick usually wears a beard, and one striking item of clothing—perhaps a red waistcoat—in an otherwise standard dress. He's the only one to say 'fucking' when girls are present. None of the working-class boys would ever do this. He's owned a series of near-vintage cars, and many times started rival bands to Tony. But whereas he is a more competent, driving trumpeter than Tony, he's not so good an organiser and doesn't melt into the landscape well enough to be as successful with publicans, club secretaries and council clerks. After ten years in the club he married a working-class girl—also an early leaver from grammar school—and moved to a better job in the Midlands. They are expected back at the club only at festival times—Easter, Whit, Christmas.

STEVE: Steve used to play the piano, but now it's gone out of fashion and he's taught himself banjo and double bass. His father was a foreman in a chemical works. He went to the grammar school, was in the 'C' stream, and had one term in the sixth form.

The school advised his parents to withdraw him, arguing that he couldn't get much more out of education. He then took a series of odd jobs—packing shoes, labouring in a market garden, until he decided to take 'A' levels and make his way to university himself. He got a job loading milk crates on the early morning carts. It was hard unpleasant work, usually done by Poles or more recent immigrants. The job started at 5 a.m. each day and ended around 3 p.m. After a short sleep, this gave him time to study before going out for a night's drinking. Slowly, over a period of years he obtained the necessary 'A' levels. Being in the 'C' stream he had not studied Latin, and so found that he could read History, without having an 'O' level Latin qualification, at Leeds or Bangor. He was accepted at Bangor, and had saved enough to pay for his first year there. The local authority gave him no support, nor did the school. But after a successful first year, Bangor worked strongly to help him raise grants and finish his degree course. He was ill for a year with tuberculosis but after being cured he returned to Bangor and got his degree. He now teaches History in a Huddersfield secondary modern school.

He is the only one of the Jazz Club who could have made a living from music by playing with one of the big bands. When the opportunity came, he went on a jazz tour of Germany, then turned the project down in favour of his university ambition. A big drinker, and vintage car expert, he is immensely popular both in the Jazz Club and with working-class drinkers at the local pub. Sometimes he wears a beard, sometimes not. When he does he changes its cut and style frequently, and talks about it a great deal. Both in the pub and at the jazz club, many stand rather in awe of him—not able to size him up. With his degree behind him his intellectual interests have largely dried up. He doesn't interest himself in politics at all, and has no ambitions as a schoolmaster. His past tenacity is no longer required, and he's thoroughly adjusted to Huddersfield life and rhythm. 'Friday's drinking night, Saturday's jazz night, and Sunday's picture night.'

TOMMY: Tommy was the band's first clarinetist, but he played so badly he was soon discarded. The others said it was because he had rheumatics in his fingers. He left grammar school at the 'O' level stage and drifted miserably from job to job—gardener, auctioneer's clerk, office-boy. Finally, he entered a mental hospital as a voluntary patient. He began to reappear gradually at the club, bringing his clarinet and sitting quietly doodling with it under the table so that nobody could hear it but himself. 'I'm digging shallow from now on, man. I've dug too deep in the past. Don't think about anything, just go on from day to day.' He doesn't talk much, but when he does, it is almost entirely in a jazz idiom. He sits, in old suit and black glasses, fairly close to the band. Sometimes he's joined there by two more, also wearing dark glasses. He is one of the few who listen to the music. For a while, when Patrick brought the art student world into the Jazz Club, he tried his hand at painting. But now he's gone back entirely to jazz as his sole world. One of the art students, with anxieties of his own, is one of the few who talk much to him—and he's continually turning over his conversations with Tommy, as if looking for clues to his own condition. 'I think jazz is a way out. I was talking to Tommy and his ideas are just the same as mine. When I'm playing jazz by myself—not when I'm with a group— that's when I can forget myself, completely. That's the only time I can forget myself. That, and running. That's partly why I took up running. When you're out running I find I can forget every-thing and that gives you a chance to start again. Things build up and build up until you feel you can't do anything. Just before Christmas I was like that. I couldn't work. I couldn't do anything. I felt the tension inside. I wanted to cry. I used to get the tension in lectures that I wanted to cry—in fact I did cry once. I ran down the stairs and I burst out crying. I couldn't stop myself. I find that most of the people who feel the same way as I do about things are verging on the border of mental. Tommy thinks much the same. Well, it's not that I think they're mental—it's what other people would say they are. His problem's much the same as mine. Our trouble is to find any point to life. We had a talk about whether suicide was the way out, but he said if that was all it came to, suicide—what was the point of suicide?'

For Tommy, the Jazz Club is the only place where he feels he has an accepted role.

A list of the Jazz Club members would very much repeat the above pattern. Almost all are boys and girls from working-class homes who went to grammar school. They have jobs in Huddersfield as clerks, or else they are struggling to get back into education —taking an external degree whilst working on the sewerage plant, looking for mature teacher training courses, or art college openings. One or two have been mental patients, one or two repeat Steve's tenacity and stick until they get somewhere. The girls come from an identical background. and usually left grammar school at fifteen or sixteen. But they are far less anxious and seldom worry about jobs or careers. They are usually typists, content to live in the present and marry when the time comes.

What is the Jazz Club?

The Jazz Club has lasted thirteen years so far. Its oldest members are in their thirties, and they joined 'the crowd' as schoolboys and schoolgirls. It began with one of the post-war generations of teenagers. Its class and educational basis appears clear enough. New members are recruited to the central group, fairly slowly— so its age range has been steadily broadening: 15 to 29, 15 to 30, 15 to 31 . . . Marriage doesn't take the older ones away, only new jobs or personal disaster does that. It's obvious what the Jazz Club is *not*. It's not a club needing the permanence of buildings and officers. It doesn't want organising, as the bus driver's failure suggested. It likes to keep together, yet keep on the move. It isn't a soft drink and coffee club. There must be beer. This cuts it off from the large audiences of grammar school girls who sometimes 'take up' a folk club or student club. As a society the Jazz Club meets as a group of drinkers most nights of the week, and always has done.

Is it a *jazz* club? It is for Tony or Tommy. With both of them jazz is involved with very private realities. Yet very few others listen to the music with much attention, even among the musicians themselves. And certainly the taste for jazz doesn't become more discriminating. All look down on rock 'n roll, skiffle, beat, pop folk, or the latest style that sweeps the top twenty. But within jazz itself, interest drifts rather than sharpens. For most of the group, jazz—even if they like it a lot—is the occasion, the setting, for their society, and not its *raison d'être*. 'But I mean, how many people come down to hear good jazz. If they want to hear really good jazz, they wouldn't come out at all. You'd stop at home and play Morton records, wouldn't you? But that's the last thing I go to the Jazz Club for. There I like it as background to all that's going on.'

But what is going on? I think that what happened originally was that a group of working-class boys at grammar school found themselves at odds with the social and academic demands of their school. 'I hated the etiquette, the sugar tongs part of it.' Yet at the same time they were excited and enthusiastic, and the colour and music of jazz and the jazz myth satisfied them in a way that the G.C.E. demands of the schoolroom never could. They fell in love with the literature of jazz too—the prostitution, violence, drugs of New Orleans went along with its music, vitality, imagination. If the life of New Orleans was an exaggerated image of working-class life, the stimulating generalised emotions of jazz were a hazy image of what the world of art could offer. The school avoided the first and didn't particularly lead to the second. The Jazz Club has ever since slowly recruited from this type of grammar school pupil. Eight years later, for example, two new members—girl and boy—discussed the school dance at the girls' grammar school.

It's like a lot of sixth formers trying to do a Billy Butlin. There are different kinds, like—there are a few couples who've come to dance, and they do. Then there are the others who're just going round the floor to see if they can knock into old so-and-so. And then there are the ones standing around. It's the band that tries to be like Butlin's too. This time there was this band leader, for example, who said "Next it'll be the Lancers, and those who aren't going to dance, should go up into the balcony and they'll see a *lovely* sight!" Well that kind of thing—it makes me sick!'

'Yes, and you can't be comfortable. You feel the mistresses are watching you. You feel you're under their eyes.'

'And no wonder some of them are "misses"? Their dresses were shocking! Perhaps they find teaching's a greater call—but what taste! Really shocking!'

'It isn't right for all the girls either. There's that lot who usually go dancing to the Masonic, and they feel it's all a bit below them. And then there's the ones who go to Chinnie's, and its all a bit too high for them.'

'What about the refreshments too. When you go to a dance, you get to wanting your refreshments and things around about nine o'clock. Or most guys do anyway. But what happened? The staff and their guests and so on had theirs then, and the room was closed to everyone. We had to stay outside until they were finished, before we could have anything.'

'Yes, I know. It was given out in Assembly before. There were special times for the Lower Sixth and for the. . . .'

'Special times! It makes you sick.'

'Oh yes, and Miss Scotland has got the Astronomer Royal to come along from a lecture he was giving earlier that evening. That was given out in Assembly too. We hadn't got to all stare and stop talking when he came in. When we got there, some of the fourth formers asked Peter if he were the Astronomer Royal.'

'I was very tempted to say yes, too!'

But the link with education seems to go rather further than this. Many of the Jazz Club members, like Steve or Patrick, had a great deal of trouble in reaching and lasting through higher education. It could take them ten years or more between leaving school and obtaining a further qualification. Taken one by one, the club's members present an astonishing variety of 'broken' educations. The club also offered securities to those on the borderlands of mental illness or suffering from other anxieties. There was always for example, an amount of only half-recognised homosexual worry. One player was always quarrelling with his mates' girl friends and at almost any moment over a ten-year period you could hear the latest girl friend of his latest mate, irritated, angry or puzzled with him say 'Why are you so hostile tonight? You always seem hostile to me.' It took him a decade to realise himself that he was homosexual, and before that very few indeed of 'the crowd' had perceived his problem. Most—despite their education and including some in a similar plight—would probably have been rather shocked.

Difficulties of this kind clustered round the jazz club but were not its centre. That remained in the entanglements of the working-class boy, having passed through grammar school, running into all manner of emotional checks from sixteen onwards. Other people were involved, but these were the centre—just as old men remain central even in a bowls club with many young or women members. The Jazz Club was a community with a fairly subtle structure. Unlike the working men's clubs it wasn't in any sense 'local'; it was inconceivable that it should have premises or a constitution, or that the instruments should be owned by the club, not the individual. Yet it was nevertheless a community, and not like the grammar school itself, simply an élite in training. It had points of resemblance to the clubs—from its informal but effective style of leadership which was quite different from the public school prefect manner, to a rather delightful insistence on the 'difficulty' of jazz which much resembled the similarly false 'difficulty' from which brass bandsmen often sought to create their mystery. But to dress in uniform, like a brass band or a top twenty beat group, was inconceivable—that was altogether too close to the ethos of grammar school.

As the Jazz Club shifted around Huddersfield for thirteen years it carried on a kind of long flirtation with the older working-class groups. There were cricket matches against mill teams—with the Jazz Club team eccentrically dressed. There were months when a very drab working-class pub was in favour because it had a pianist who played popular songs of the twenties and thirties ('Jack Dempsey')—with which 'the crowd' characteristically, were more word-perfect than the labourers who used the pub. There was a long adoption of an outlying pub where the choir gathered round the bar after evening service and part-sang spirited Methodist hymns ('Crown Him') in between pints. 'The crowd' all knew the 'Huddersfield Anthem'—'Pretty Flowers'—a lovely Napoleonic broadside, of which the rest of Huddersfield knows only the first line and a vague patch of its soaring melody. And there were several attempts at setting up comic Edwardian song acts on the working men's club circuits. It was a love affair. The Jazz Club—despite the New Orleans myth and the educational background—was very much a Huddersfield club. It didn't lead to social promotion or to high art—there was no 'transfer' at all from jazz to classical music. Its function was to hold together and sustain a steady stream of post-1944 Act pupils. As a floating community, it became admirably and intricately designed for that purpose—and the feeling of how to do *this*, was the real inheritance from working-class Huddersfield.

Chapter Nine

SCHOOL ENDS

Focusing Out

At four o'clock the girls from Silveredge High begin to spread down the slight hill from school and into the city centre. First come the twos and threes of very young girls, running for the early buses. They shout a lot and push for good places in the short queues. White ankle socks, dark-blue uniform, dark-blue berets hurriedly scrambled on; sometimes bright yellow rulers poke out of new satchels. The first buses pull out, conductors hanging on the platform, anxious to be away with a light teatime load before the coming crowd of grammar school children pack the seats. By now there's a thick drift of dark-blue uniforms coming down the hill, and the bus queues form quickly again, with small groups of Silveredge girls separated by handfuls of adults. The girls are full of chatter, absorbed in each other: intervening adults hardly exist. At the head of the queue an isolated workman, worn flat cap, shaven grey hair, puffs at a stubby pipe and stares at the pigeons perched on Ackroyd's roof gutters. The queues lengthen, but still with these erratic divisions between schoolgirls and shoppers. The women shoppers hardly talk, but brood over the girls, taking in the streams of enclosed chatter, even down to the way one girl says the algebra homework should be done. Twice an excited girl turns too quickly round and knocks against a shopping basket, apologises with embarrassment and is lost once more in the schoolgirl talk. The women smile quickly, on-and-off, say 'It's quite all right', and keep their baskets where they were.

The 4.10 buses come in. The workman climbs slowly to the upper deck, still absorbed. The shoppers settle downstairs, spreading themselves and their parcels over the seats. The school-girls flow on board, courteous and careful, despite the conductor who channels them, hurries-them-on-please, bars and unbars the way. At first the girls scramble a little, snatching at the empty double-seats, guarding them for friends. The last girls perch alongside shoppers, excluded by distance and manners from further conversation until the end of the run. The buses draw out with no delay. A further one is already coming in, another queue forming.

By 4.20 the first spurt away from school is over, and again there is only a scatter of blue uniforms coming down the hill. But these are older girls—fifteen, sixteen, seventeen, eighteen, walking more slowly, more self-consciously. Under the chemist's clock four or five girls—all about sixteen—are talking to boys from the grammar school. Berets have been stuffed in pockets and satchels. This is the recognised meeting place—just far enough from Silver-edge to be recognised, by girls and by teachers, as out of the school's sway and belonging to the public centres of life. A mistress passes: the talking stops, and four girls stare challengingly —the fifth contemplates the clock. The boys and girls could easily meet in a more secluded place, such as Thompson's shopping arcade where they go on rainy days—but Monday to Friday, year after year, they cluster here.

The last group of girls pass the half-dozen under the clock: glance, glance again, and say nothing. No one now is in any hurry to get home; but yet the girls take very different directions. Two or three trios of sixth formers are making for the public library, for a gossip in the Foreign Language corner, far from the assistant's desk. For one or two, there will be a grammar school boy waiting on the library steps. Four or five fifth-form girls, following them, turn off for the Santa Maria—a teenage coffee bar. Bright blue neon lights, already lit, point the way up a disused yard between the shoe shops. Girls from Glossop Road, St. John's, Aggridge and Park End secondary modern schools will soon be at the 'Santa', together with the odd office junior slipping in for ten minutes instead of delivering letters—and then, after five o'clock, boys from the mills and engineering works.

By 4.30 the dark-blue uniforms have almost disappeared, and the first men and women are breaking from the factories, stepping it out to catch their own 'first bus'.

This is the scene on most school evenings of the year. Everyone in Huddersfield knows the Silveredge uniform, knows the tone and manners that are said to go with it. There are boys and girls from secondary modern schools passing through the centre at tea-time; but in their everyday assortment of clothes, or new and unestablished uniforms, they seem anonymous, and never catch the Huddersfield eye. The Silveredge girls are distinct. The shoppers and the bus conductor recognise and envy the 'manners', and at the same time they want to hustle them, draw them out of their own private into the public world—'hurry along, *please*' . . . 'it's quite all right'.

They are part of the Huddersfield scene, and about half of them come from working-class homes; generally the daughters of very skilled men, seldom of the unskilled. 'One or two of their fathers work at Cartwrights, or play in the bands. You sometimes see the girls in the park whilst watching the old men at bowls. They came to the Jazz Club at its most popular moments, but didn't become part of it. For some the life of kin and neighbourhood, of club, mill, band, union or chapel is going to be the life led not only by their parents but by those of their brothers and sisters who did not pass for grammar school.

This is how the girls look to me. But how does Huddersfield look to them, how do they see the society in which they live? How do they feel about growing up inside that unique dark-blue uniform? In order to sketch in a little of the answer, we asked the staff at Silveredge to invite a group of 15- and 16-year-old girls to write freely on 'Growing up in Huddersfield'. The following account is based on thirty-four such essays. It was realised that these essays might produce many merely 'formal' and 'expected' accounts; and so the girls were told the pieces were not for the staff but for total strangers, that they would not be marked in any way, that real names need not be used—and above all, they were asked to be candid. But naturally you don't get candid prose merely by asking for it. The girls inevitably test out this attitude and that, without being fully conscious of it; in-evitably, they confuse the second-hand and the merely 'polite' with the fresh and personal. Yet the degree of frankness attained, and the quality of intelligence at work in their writing, is in its way as useful a comment on the life of Silveredge school as any of the overt quotations which follow.

Exit from Childhood

To begin with many of the girls described the difficult emotional flux of adolescence. They wrote about how, along with the new excitement, had come malaise and depression—moods in which Huddersfield seemed a shabby backcloth to their forlorn identity.

'I begin to wonder what was the point of it all, why were people living on this earth? Why was I who I am? At these times Huddersfield seems to be an extremely dirty town and very miserable. Especially with the rain and the fog, the dull monotony of the daily routine, the miserable feeling of being alone—life in Huddersfield then feels hardly bearable. At one time I was even getting to the point of hating school, but now I seem to be emerging from that slough.'

They know what has to be expected from adolescence, but against this has to be placed the seeming fickleness of adults:

'They treat us like children, and expect us to behave in a mature, adult fashion. Parents say that "moods", especially of elation quickly followed by depression, are all part of growing up. What they do not seem to realise is that they cause these moods especially when we feel depressed and miserable by their constant nattering and criticism.'

At home the turbulent angers at being treated now as a child, now as adult, can burst into open, but equally perplexing argument:

'Obviously the main problems of my growing up is the relationship between myself and my parents. These fluctuate considerably between being told "You don't know what you're talking about", and that I am "careless beyond all measure", to being complimented on my logic by my father when I have got the better of a discussion with my mother.'

But this varied from girl to girl, and some felt that in general they lived as adults on Saturday and Sunday, but as children at Silveredge on the other five days:

'Home life is not punctuated with noisy rows and deadly silences. There, at least, one is accepted as a more adult person and treated as such. At school, however, this is not so. During the week one is treated as a child, as one in a crowd, with no personality or feelings.

The mere thought of wearing a beret because three hundred other girls do, fills me with something more than annoyance. This appears to be a major problem, the difficulty of changing back into a schoolgirl after two days of being "grown up"—and having to return to school uniform again.'

On the other hand, a few—especially from middle class backgrounds—felt differently and were satisfied by the tokens of coming maturity they received at school:

'I think my main problem has been trying to catch up with the girls that have grown up before me, and who do not approve of my too childish behaviour and hairstyle. They keep telling me that "everyone is clamping down on us" at schools, that we need more freedom, more responsibility, and that we should not be treated like children. Personally, apart from righteous anger at the occasional stupidities and unfair judgments of the staff (not always concerning myself), I find in school as much freedom and happiness as I wish. I enjoy being in the sixth form for the childish reason that I can use the front door, wear a skirt, and answer the telephone.'

But what didn't vary very much from girl to girl was the sense that either parents or teachers might at any time knock them back into childhood by snatching away the adult respects and responsibilities that the girls felt they needed:

'At one time I am told to remember that I am now nearly seventeen, and that it is time I realised that I was growing up; and then soon after I am told that I must do this, do that, conform to this regulation and abide by that law. Naturally it is very pleasing when people tell us we are growing up, and give responsibility, but the next moment when you are treated like a child, it is most upsetting.'

From these pressures the girls often turn aside into inner worlds of fantasy: 'I often allow myself to lapse into dreams' says one girl. 'I am normally very active' continues another,

'But sometimes I am just in the mood to think, and I have to sort myself out. Sometimes, when I am just thinking, my mother or someone else tells me I am just wasting time and ask what it can be that needs so much thought. I think that because older people have already taken their place, and presumably accepted it, they tend to take it for granted and cannot understand that we have yet to do this.'

Many girls mentioned private thinking into religion, and

though here and there this seemed no more than a polite recognition of an 'expected' subject, there were some for whom it seemed a very real part of these adolescent turmoils. Pauline Duce brings to her religion fears and doubts that are hardly tamed by rational enquiry:

> 'As a child I often had nightmares about the existence of the world, going on and on and on—until I had to stop thinking about it. The grammar school gave me a new approach to these problems, especially the broadcasts in the sixth form. I began to think more profoundly at my being at all, and thought up reasonable answers for my own questions. Some of my problems concerning death were solved for me by books the minister lent after discussions with him, but still I have problems about the ultimate end of the world— whether it will come by nuclear war, or by Act of God.'

Other girls, almost with a sense of surprise at the sceptical thrust of their own intelligence, find their childhood securities suddenly displaced:

> 'I begin to wonder why on earth God should send his son to a tiny speck of dust such as us. I suppose this is trying to fit in scientific fact with religion and sometimes unfortunately I cannot. I begin to question whether Jesus was God's son, or whether he was merely a man with greater than average powers who thought he was the son of God. And then I wonder why, if Moslems and Buddhists think theirs is a true religion, why should ours be the only true one. Sometimes I even wonder if there really is a God at all.'

And others like Brenda Drysdale know very clearly what is personal and what, for them, merely belongs to formal school training:

> 'Religion has its problems and at the moment I am in the throes of deciding whether I am agnostic or atheist. Of course, practically everyone who has been through the mill of the sixth form knows all the arguments on the subject, and they are not worth repeating here. I am too unfeeling and inquisitive to be religious.'

Comments like these on the difficulties of adolescence, the changing moods, the new discovery of identity, the withdrawals into self, and the perplexities in finding and holding the social role of an adult, could of course be found elsewhere. These are general and inevitable problems, and played their own part, though with a different 'feel', in the Jazz Club. But how do these Silveredge girls that we see on the streets feel about growing up in *Huddersfield*, and the world that is discussed in the previous chapters? What do they value in the city, and what does it lack?

Exit from Community

In writing about their town, many advanced the formal claims that are made each evening in the local paper: that Huddersfield is a famous sporting city, that it is an internationally famous musical centre, that it is surrounded by beautiful countryside, and so on. A more dispassionate authority, Niklaus Pevsner, finds the city's architecture to be generally undistinguished. The Town Hall built in times of High Victorian prosperity, he judges 'ornate and debased', though he picks out the railway station, a dignified Corinthian composition of 1847 with long low wings, as 'one of the best early railway stations in England'. Most of the girls would disagree with him. Visually, they don't look at Huddersfield like this. Nary Wallis, for instance, writes:

'There are some nice places here, the Town Hall is beautiful, but the outside of the Station and the George Hotel are an eyesore. They ought to be cleaned up. They look absolutely disgusting.'

Similarly many girls selected the public library for special architectural mention, though Pevsner ignores it completely. It was clearly enough the *social* significance of the library which lay behind their architectural comment. (Just as the girl above was seeing the Town Hall not as a civic office, but as a very grand dance-hall, which it is on Saturday nights.) Indeed, in one way or another, more girls mentioned the library than anything else, though often enough, in talking about its contents, they added to the formal claim in illuminating ways:

'There is a very good public library. The most useful section is the reference library, and quite a pleasant afternoon can be spent looking at the books. The reference library has copies of past G.C.E. papers, and these are very helpful in showing the kinds of questions asked.'

Others spoke favourably of the city's parks, and one or two gave their attention not to the library, but to more 'superior' buildings. Sybil Sharp, for example, discussed the merits and shortcomings of Huddersfield's most expensive hotels, and concluded:

'There are only two decent hotels, the 'George' which is a four star hotel in the A.A. book, and the 'Queen' which is only a three star hotel. I feel there should be at least one five star.'

But most of these girls did not talk in terms of A.A. books and four star hotels. They were more immediately interested in teenage outlets in Huddersfield, and after discussing the most prominent buildings in Huddersfield, the visual background to their argument became not Corinthian stations or grand hotels, but coffee bars, dance halls, street corners, the market place at weekends. The basic difficulty was that most of them could not discover a teenage world that they could accept, and they were left with that hollow gap between the school debating society and the symphony concert in the Town Hall. They wanted brightness and gaiety, the excitements of young people together, but these could be difficult to discover. Often enough they mentioned the need for more coffee bars 'as there are some cafés, but most of these are taken up by adults'. This was interesting because there are several coffee bars in Huddersfield, but this was not what the Silveredge girls wanted—indeed they disapproved of the people who used them. They wanted new, *selective*, coffee bars for themselves and the grammar school boys. Similarly, several asked for fresh youth clubs where they 'could meet and make as much noise as required'. Again there were many flourishing youth clubs in the town, but once more they disliked the people who used them. They wanted their *own* youth clubs. Many of the older girls who wandered around the public library at teatime and then retired for a full evening's homework, would have delighted in a kind of superior coffee bar life, but not for anything would they have turned off into the 'Santa Maria'.

But there were some of these girls who had already broken with the social life and decorums that the school years seemed to enforce. Where others wrote of the formal claims to be made for Huddersfield, and more personally of its library and countryside, these girls wrote of boy friends, dance halls, public houses. Wendy Young, rightly or wrongly, felt that Silveredge frowned on boy friends:

139

'Growing up is very difficult from my point of view because I attend an all girls' school where it is considered a small sin to be seen meeting a boy in your school uniform. If we are seen about Huddersfield by a member of the staff and we have a lot of make-up on, we are likely to be reprimanded at school the following week, that is even though we don't wear make-up at school.'

To Wendy, school, its societies and its homework, are not the only reality. Most of her pages describe her week-end life, and for her this obviously *is* 'life', and school, like homework, a 'disadvantage' to be endured.

'Besides the disadvantages which are evident during the week, there are the disadvantages of having quite a lot of homework, which restricts the number of times a week that one can go out. I go out three nights a week—Friday, Saturday and Sunday. On Fridays I go to the Youth Club, but I don't really enjoy myself there because there are no facilities for girls and the only things to do are "jive" or play table tennis. On Saturday I work and because of this I am not altogether liked by the headmistress. She thinks girls should get as much fresh air as possible at weekends. On Saturday evenings I arrive home from work about six-thirty and if I am going dancing I leave home again about eight. On Sundays my friends and I usually go to a coffee bar which is regarded by the older people as being quite a den of iniquity—that is just because the younger people congregate there. I don't go to church on a Sunday at all because church has nothing to offer me, and my parents don't force me to go. Don't think I'm an atheist and have never seen the inside of a church, because I used to go every Sunday evening until I became bored. Up until recently the public houses in Huddersfield only stayed open until 10 p.m., but the magistrates decided to alter it to 10.30 p.m. I think that along with this they should alter the age at which young people can enter a public house.'

Cynthia Ker also belonged to this small, dissident group, and she too is attracted by pubs.

'I am no angel and I don't criticise people, because I myself have done just about everything I shouldn't. Like most teenagers I smoke. I have also been drinking, but this is not uncommon in Huddersfield, and I have found it amazing the number of people who drink under eighteen. In the local paper every day there is some criticism of the teenager, and I have heard that the Town Council are thinking of building a floral hall. They might do some good if they built a Youth Centre instead of building something that will hardly be seen after the first week. It is a useless waste of money. Growing up in Huddersfield was quite pleasant until I realised that many places have far more activities, and choice of activities.'

A third member of this group is Mary Wallis. She says that she would like 'to earn some money and be more independent, so that I could afford to go to the more expensive places in town.' But as it is she seems, unlike almost all the other Silveredge girls, quite happy mixing in with the general teenage life of the city:

'I go to Charlie Frost's of which most older people don't approve because it is modern dancing and it is quite dark. There is nothing whatsoever to disapprove of, because there is nothing wrong with the things that go on. The teenagers just enjoy themselves without having to obey a lot of hard and fast rules about whether they should smoke, etc. When we are left alone we are not rowdy; it is only when we are ordered about that we want to rebel and cause trouble.'

The girls seem to break up into a larger and a smaller group. The small group is made up of girls who respond to the excited impulses of adolescence by breaking away from school and trying their hand at adult work, and by joining in the general adolescent life of the city. A little frightened, and quite illegally, they explore the pubs. More confidently, and yet conscious of unspoken social prohibitions, they mix in at coffee bars, jazz clubs, dance halls, with that other teenage population of Huddersfield—a population which is socially working-class, and educationally, secondary modern. Most of the girls who act like this come themselves from working-class homes; very likely they will not stay much longer at Silveredge. School is an interruption.

The majority of their class mates looked on at this social life, but drew back. For them there were school societies, the Guide troop, the church—though none wrote with excitement about any of these. Or they could join in the fringes of middle class social life, by attending the week-end concert ('but I think that's a waste of a *Saturday* night'), or the chamber recitals in the Mayor's Parlour. Or they could stand on the sidelines waiting to become part of another middle-class life—the social world of expensive dinner dances and four star hotels. They certainly glanced in these directions, yet what they wrote about most of all was a world which they couldn't enter easily—exclusively teenage, full of colour, noise, music, boy friends. Others found this in the youth clubs and coffee bars, and the Silveredge girls badly wanted all this, and yet wanted it to be selective ('no Irish youths and teddy boys') and superior ('with perhaps a cabaret'). Their desires and turbulent high spirits were deflected back to the guides, the church, the library and the long homework hours.

Community into Élite

It seems reasonable to suggest that the demand for a selective youth club and coffee bar culture of their own was connected with their own selective education, with their apartness in their distinctive dark-blue uniforms from the majority of Huddersfield children. Twenty to twenty-five per cent of the town's pupils see how the Silveredge girls wrote about education, and about the seventy-five or eighty per cent who attended the secondary modern schools.

Jennifer Priest, for instance, drew into her discussion the expected 'decorums' of the grammar school girl:

'Having been brought up in a grammar school, one is expected by now to be able to appreciate the beauties of the flower beds in the parks, and not have to rush around letting steam off.'

Rosemary Ludman, just as naturally, observes the decorums in her friendships with boys. After explaining her difficulties in finding places to go because 'most dance halls are of a low class', and 'the coffee bars and cafés are also mainly of the low class type', she considers whether a grammar school girl of fifteen or sixteen may reasonably go out with boys 'in a sensible and decent manner'. She concludes that she may, but adds a proviso:

'Obviously, if a boy desires your company, *providing he is a decent educated boy*, it is only human nature to accept his offer.'

Alison King is similarly troubled about where to meet and to accompany boy-friends, how to find 'a place where decent, sociable young people go'. To her most of the teenage population of Huddersfield are teddy boys and teddy girls: 'Not all of them are the murderous type, but they certainly are not of very high class, because they would have been brought up better.' She decides that in the end she prefers her weekly 'ten shilling riding lesson' to any of the town's attractions. As with many of her friends, 'decent' and 'respectable' comes as automatic words in her vocabulary for social relationships.

Caroline Harvey sometimes talks to girls from the secondary modern but, much against her sense of the proper dignities of teenage conversations, she discovers that one subject only controls discussion:

'Going to a grammar school I look on others with a biased view, but those girls in my own form seem more mature to me than girls who have been to other schools. And I find it difficult to carry on a conversation with people outside Silveredge without coming round to the topic of boys.'

Not all girls seem to have her contacts, and again and again many of them write as if all other teenagers in Huddersfield were hooligans or 'scruffs': the teddy boy stereotype expands to cover most of the ex-secondary modern population. Some girls were extremely candid about this sense of where they stood in relation to others:

'Some people in this town are not as clean as they should be, and I think policemen ought to have the right to wash people's faces and necks if they feel like it.'

But however they felt about the remainder of the teenage population from which they were set apart, it was these others who dominated the coveted coffee bars. Some consoled themselves with the lonely solace of homework:

'All my evenings (sometimes nights too) are taken up with home-work and private extra study. This work appears endless and I emerge from a "session" weak, helpless. The coffee bars and snack bars etc., are the main congregating grounds for other teenagers, but I personally do not patronise these establishments, preferring to drink hot Nescafé at home rather than cool insipid liquid to the blaring of a juke box at eightpence a time in a howling hole of humanity.'

But the general picture was sharply defined—most longed for some of the excitement of the other world.

'Youth clubs are *all right for some people*' said Margaret Braith-waite. 'I think more coffee bars should be opened so that one could *go with a particular set of friends* and not practically the whole youth of Huddersfield.'

No doubt most of the middle-class girls had always felt 'apart' from the rest of the population, even before they went to Silveredge. But two girls from working-class homes chose to write about the way they had once belonged to the more inclusive community, but now at sixteen they felt themselves divorced, members of an élite—and glad of it. Pauline Duce put it most directly:

'I can't say that my life changed completely on entering the secondary school except that going out to play with friends had to be put off till after homework. Perhaps I did not feel the change, because I still had a cross-section of friends from secondary moderns and other secondary selection schools. One by one those friends dwindled away, until my band of friends only included those from this school and from the church I attended. Problems did not come from my friendships, but from within the family. Quarrels with my parents usually arise from the fact that other children are earning their living at my age—why can't I be a bit more thoughtful. Usually the replies are—you sent me to grammar school and I can't help you a lot because of my homework. Most of the problems are connected with this—how to help my parents and yet how to continue with my work. Grammar school taught me to read widely, yet at the expense of my parents. I thought an evening could not be spent in a pleasanter way than doing my homework and then reading—and not joining in conversation but when spoken to, to quit.

'In early adolescence when I was with my non-grammar school friends I was well satisfied with detective novels or a "funny" film and "pop music", but now I have learnt to appreciate finer things such as real music and more subtle entertainments. Previously I had to go to a cinema for my entertainment but walks and hikes give me more thrills. I still feel excited when I see natural things on these walks, such as foxes and rabbits and marvellous views.

'At school we are urged to have a fuller education and then serve the country because it has served you, etc., and devote your life to having a career not a family. This creates a problem— whether to want to get married on leaving university or have a career and help the world and one's parents. These are the problems I have had to face in the so-called process of growing. Many of the problems I think are created by people who are now grown up, and are a lot of fuss about nothing—such as the eleven-plus examinations.'

It would be a delicate matter to fully analyse in Pauline's prose the subtle shift of cultures, the vital impulses of intelligent growth crossed by the merely 'formal' attitudes, and by social pressures which blank out her responsiveness in some areas as they enlarge it in others. But is there no other way for a Silveredge girl to come to terms with Huddersfield? Must they either damp down their other impulses and accept only the Public Library as their social centre? Or choosing to join in the life of the 'Santa Maria' must they prepare to leave Silveredge? Or like Pauline, crossing from one world to another, have they to leave all behind? Only one, in an embarrassed note, claimed to get the best out of both worlds.

This was Ellery Squires whose social centre was neither the public library nor a coffee bar, but the Jazz Club. She has the decorous conscience of the true Silveredge girl, but its meek voice is hardly strong enough to restrain those desires for a turbulent social life that Silveredge usually chastens:

'There is for me a tremendous struggle between what I suppose is my conscience and my own personal "devil". For instance, when I go to a party, while I am there I could not care less what I do, but when I wake up the following morning I begin to wonder if what I did was right or wrong. I think I have an over-active conscience, which is a nuisance, for some of the things over which I feel uncomfortable do not matter in the least.

'I like jazz because somehow it seems to express everything that's bottled up inside me, and jiving gives me a change to let myself go for a change without people frowning down their noses. It's funny that I don't care what neighbours or older people think, but when it's a question of people my own age it matters, too much. I hope you never find out who wrote this. I've never written such terrible English. It sounds very much like a little girl of about thirteen.'

The girls who come down the hill from Silveredge go their different ways—to meet boys under the chemist's clock, to sit over coffee, to congregate for a cosy hour in the public library. They share the many emotional lifts and dips of adolescents anywhere else, and cast longingly around them for that securely adult status which is so elusive. About Huddersfield itself they are formally proud, but sharp and resentful because it makes little physical provision for their moment of life. Between the Girl Guides and the symphony concert, between church choir and a four star hotel, is an unfilled adolescent gap. Something of a distinct teen-age culture has imposed itself on the city, especially in the form of youth clubs and coffee bars and perhaps the Jazz Club, but it is not for them. The Silveredge girls are an élite in training, and this part of the training comes especially hard. For the high spirits and sexual drives of adolescence direct their attention out-wards to the life that other young people lead. Sex seems very muted. The Silveredge tone and manner, the preparation for academic distinction and service to the country, are broken by longing glances towards the world of dance hall, jazz club, coffee bar. Their frustrations are consoled by the reminder that this other world is inhabited by boys and girls of poor unbringing, education, character and future. And yet, like many of us, they still want something that the others have.

Chapter Ten

CHANGE AND COMMUNITY

I began with the problems of community: and along with it a curiosity about the directness of response. Both qualities—the personal and the social—were present in the *Voices*, even at their harshest. From then, this book has picked up the scattered strands of a general enquiry into working-class life. The aim has been to take a series of local situations and to think through them, rather than through concepts. If you like, it's a working-class approach to a working-class problem: the method attuned to the pith and logic of the 'voices'.

The account of the *Mill* was a study of the frustration of community. The work was hard, the mill rooms cramped, dirty and intensely noisy. Hours were long and fluctuating: overtime was compulsory. Promotion did not exist, except for a lonely figure like Fred Beaumont, sweating out a heatwave in his jacket and tie. The only escape was to go to another factory. Inevitably some mills became—like London's East End—the places where new arrivals (Poles, West Indians) began their long climb, and where those who had dropped back (physically or mentally impaired, or simply demoralised) gradually gathered. Almost everyone at Cartwrights knew that the mill faced them at 7.30 every weekday morning for the rest of their lives. Yet at a first glance this looked like a community, not just an assortment of men and women at work. There was the constant joking, the gatherings in the lavatories or the soot-flecked corner on summer days, the free physical contact, the touching and stroking of cloth, the seaside trips. A constant reaching-out for the communal marked the natural style of life. But the workpeople had not become a community strong enough to bargain with the management. There was no union, only the longing for one. Organisers had gravitated to more pleasant mills. The management had the initiative, and by establishing a piece-work system rather than a weekly wage system, they had emphasised the divisions against the work-people. The local men were suspicious of the Poles and West Indians: a suspicion intensified because piece-work made everyone not workmates but competitors ('you can't *afford* to help other people'). Management sought productivity by playing on fissures within the community. The workpeople reacted by using their own weapons. Since overtime was compulsory, and work hours bore no relation to the rest of their interests and responsibilities, they earned high wages for a number of days, then took a day off and spent it sleeping, or bowling in the park or sitting in the club. Management's term for this was 'absenteeism', and it was re-garded—in an uncomprehending way—as a moral failing. We can see this simple ethic being transmitted to the schools in the morning assembly leaflet on 'laziness'.

A second defence set up by the work people was 'rate-fixing'. Again, management regarded the 'fiddle book' as immoral. But the 'fiddle' was part of the shadow thrown by the piece-work system. Once more, failure to understand the group resulted in a tenacious blockage in production. Management was anonymous (the owner's name not generally known) and both distant and baffling in its bureaucratic structure ('but that assistant has an assistant, and he's got an assistant').[1] Successive alterations to the piece-rates only produced a kind of busy standing-still. So far as production was concerned they had no more effect than a television appeal by the Prime Minister. And for the same reason. They tried to impose an action on the assumption that middle class life was normal life, and working-class life only a problem variant. But before management could hope to reach its economic aims it would have had to understand the closely personal, intricately-linked and sharply limited community it was dealing with. The communal urge could then have been harnessed for a common good. I take the illustration of productivity to show the practical help that can flow from an understanding of the otherness of working-class life, and from a readiness to accept that it might

[1] For an American report on a lengthy strike resulting from a breakdown between the primary group among the workpeople and the bureaucratic chain of management, see Warner, W. L. and Low, J. O. *The Social System of the Modern Factory* (1947).

have enduring strengths. But there are more fully human grounds than those.

In contrast, the study of *Working's Men's Clubs* emerged as a community in action. The clubs are co-operative societies engaged in buying and selling beer. They depend upon the familiar elaboration of kinship and neighbourhood ties. They offer seclusion and rest from the noise of the mill and the demands of home: games, newspapers, papers, and above all conversation. Like pubs they provide a social centre, but without the same pressure to drink—they are just as open to the teetotaller and the pensioner. Unlike pubs, they give the drinker a weapon against the brewery chains and their advertising machines: the clubs are islands of free choice within monopolies. And like some pubs, they sprout other activities—treats for children, help for the old, encouragement for sick or injured workmates. Their limitations are expressed—like the mill—when they meet unexpected or strange groups. The closest of these is working-class women. ('We used to have a nice little room at the back for women, with a wireless'.) More strange are coloured immigrants. No club excludes them: it hardly needs to, since the entrance procedure may baffle the immigrant. But if a West Indian or Pakistani does apply, he is accepted. Whether more would be accepted or not is hard to say, but if one is looking for practical applications of social knowledge then it's very possible that whereas the Mill intensified the barrier between the local people and the new arrivals, the clubs could play a big part in integrating immigrant and community. The chance might come through the small group of men, still mysterious to us, who quietly lead the clubs. They have a special style of leadership: a style that may be all but invisible to someone attuned to hierarchic, 'public school' dominance.

The study of *Bowls* picked up one of the interests within the working men's clubs. Some mills had bowling teams, some working men's clubs had bowling sections: apart from this inter-lock, bowls usually stood on its own. In the bowls club, the green replaced the bar. Like the clubs, the world of bowls held a strain of muted idealism ('It provides not only physical health but moral force'): the old nonconformist energy was still alive as it is in the unions, the co-op and the labour party. But the special achieve-

ment of bowls was to provide a place for the retired man. Retirement for a working man is automatic and sudden, his body is
more physically used-up, his home—dominated for so long by
'mum'—less easily accommodates him. Bowls gives him both
activity and company, which is not confined to the old: the greens
are full of young men and he may compete and excel against teams
from his old mill. And it gives him an activity which is held in
esteem. This was a very special setting for the old: the smooth
running of the woods, the brilliance of the green, the sense of
'stage' and audience.

You could trace a line through Huddersfield marking the point
where the gap showed between middle-class and working-class
life. In the mill it was there in the wage structure and the chain
of authority, in the clubs we saw it in the planning authorities'
letter, with bowls it was present in the divergence between the
books on the library shelves and the style of bowls played here,
and again in the council's approach to bowls in municipal parks.
All these activities rested on the kinship and neighbourhood network, and by making drastic alterations to that (for example, in
terms of rehousing) an authority could destroy 'social capital' that
would be very difficult and sometimes impossible to replace.

At Bradley working men's club there was not only an interest
in bowls but a brass band practising in the cellar. And at first
sight, a study of *Brass Bands* looked a more exciting extension of
community outside the circles of the clubs. The bands were a
brilliant flash in a public rhetoric that had survived the first wave
of television. They might still be part of the gay ceremonial of
working-class life for a new generation which didn't surrender to
television as a compelling novelty, but treated it as a common
fact. Again the bands voiced the latent idealism of the community,
almost in terms of aspiration towards a musical commonwealth.
('Sincere attempt to apprehend the good, the beautiful, the true'.)
And they re-directed attention at the leadership group. This fitted
the pattern of the previous studies: so did the now familiar line
between the classes, noted here in the gap between the strong
band movement and the music of schools and civic sponsorship.
The reverse of this, and it has not had the stress it deserves, was
that in each of these studies so far, the much-discussed impact of
the media was apparently slight. The very resilience of band

music in an age of pop songs warns us against a too-simple model of society and the channels through which its interests, excitements or information are transmitted. Yet for all this, the bands were the most narrowly-based of the groups so far considered. They had not made that necessary marriage with the locality through the clubmen. They were often based not on kinship and neighbourhood, but on kinship alone. This narrowness had increased with the rise of the contest men—bringing with them a more private, if markable, music and damaging the old club loyalties by borrowing and poaching. So far these studies have been relating mill, club, bowls and band, to a fabric of home, kin and neighbourhood. But just as important is the relationship between the groups which are local, and those organisations like the co-op or the Labour party which at some point move from a prime interest in the local to a prime interest in the national. That exact point, along with the previous matter of 'leadership', is a major question for further research. The suggestion is that unions or churches or Labour party, not only attune dominantly to the national—but fail, as the bands fail, to root themselves broadly enough in the neighbourhood.

Bands, Bowls and *Clubs* offered generally positive accounts of community; *Riot* was a negative image. If we are troubled at working-class ambivalence towards the educated, or unreadiness to welcome the Pole or West Indian in the mill, we might put those dilemmas into proportion by considering the much tougher refusal to accept into the community that most familiar image of the British scene, the policeman. But this just wasn't a class riot; it was an outbreak of the young. The trouble arose from the apprentices. They came from working-class homes and neighbourhoods, they were educated at secondary modern schools like the one that offered the morning sermon on 'Laziness'. This time the binding force was not so strongly related in kinship, though no doubt that was there. Venn Street and Kirkgate filled with groups of 'mates', the peer groups that bind the young, as the bowling club binds the old. The Huddersfield riot expresses defiance of the young before they accept that their father's lot is still, in large measure, theirs too. Both the general working-class hostility to the police, and the special impulsive expression of it by the young, look fairly commonplace. All the more reason therefore why we should attend to the different explanations offered by the 'old' middle class of officials, civic heads, churchmen and the local press—and by the 'new' middle class of the metropolitan editor, his photographers and journalists. We see the 'old' middle class searching around through categories of the past—'under the influence'—to less familiar ones of the present—'race' and 'the Bomb'. Yet the journalists' thinking did not involve any attempt to understand, as the Chief Constable's genuinely did. They tried on a set of accepted news slots—sex, violence, race, drugs, beatniks—until a serviceable one was found. The news slots did not come from the rioting scene at all, they were drawn from the set of formulae and conventions that were in the structure of the mass-circulation paper itself. Moreover, after the original riots, the presence of the newsmen was a function of the news. They didn't just report it—in a catalytic way, they helped to make it. One might ponder the sense of 'stage' in the last riots, with that different sense of 'stage' which was such an important part of the old men playing bowls on the green.

Jazz Club too showed us a peer group rather than the denser sociality of the club, mill or band. But *Jazz Club* was a peer group, as it were, in suspension: a group of schoolfriends supporting each other during a decade that was very difficult for most of them. Grammar school had loosened their ties with the local community. But the grammar school experience had been double-headed. The social style and values repelled them, and many of them were 'early leavers'. Yet at the same time the school had transmitted intimations of possible experiences—especially through art and music—that eluded them. The school was in contact with intensities of living that the working-class community did not offer: but to these pupils the school hadn't—perhaps couldn't—pass them on. So most of the boys had aspirations that weren't satisfied. With some, this produced the long attempts at self-advancement, like Steve's climb to university; with others the pressure brought mental and sexual troubles out into the open, at least within the Club. Closely related to this pattern of unsatisfied social and vocational desires, was the private concern with emotional realisation, stirred by their glimpses of music and paintings. Listening to the band play, one saw that it was only a 'band' in an external sense. Each player was there to

explore his personal world. That's partly why the solos—'breaks'
—were so very important to the player and so unimportant to
his colleagues. The members had individual, almost anarchic,
needs that might have fragmented the group into thirty individuals all going their own way. The Club worked because they
also needed each other, and because in a dozen ways, they inherited and remoulded a working-class pattern of community. In
their tense situation they drew, unwittingly, on that reserve which
was the subject of earlier chapters. The little glimpses of the
police, of the newspapers, tell us something. So does the perpetual
oddity of the cash tills and the entrance fees which no one paid:
everyone felt they were 'inside'. Behind them was a background
of club membership and club building as an extension of family
life; there was the direct habit of acting out one's role within a
group, rather than dealing with life only as an individual; there
was the multitude of lines into the local community, from
seaside trips to hymn singing in the pub after church; and there
were the stabilising figures—like Tony—who could just as easily
and as quietly, run a large working men's club. *Jazz Club*, like
Riot, belongs to that picture of the new society for the young
which came after the war and the 1944 Education Act: teenage
spending and fresh importance in the economy; teenage style
and self-consciousness—and underneath, a very ancient tension
between the young and the old. At the very least the Jazz Club
supported its members through a long hard time, often prevented
them from becoming bitter in their frustration, or from being
an insupportable burden to parents, employers and the social
services. Possibly it did more. It drew a steadying strength from
the working-class background: but it kept open a line of experience which that community could not offer. For these pupils,
it sometimes did this job better than school.

School completed a trio of studies of the young working-class
boys and girls. With it the community of the earlier chapters
retreated to the distance, the speaking voices ended. We met what
to some was the exit from community, and to others just the
normal middle class style of living which they had known from
birth. The Huddersfield depicted here is the Huddersfield of the
teachers, employers, civil servants, administrators: a city of
suburbs and prosperous homes that I haven't attempted to

recreate, a city which makes claim for itself as a centre of orchestral and choral music not of brass bands and jazz; a city from which a fast car takes you in a few minutes to steak and scampi restaurants on the moors or in the dales.

Although many of the girls came from upper working-class homes, and some had relatives who were weavers in the mills like Cartwrights or who drank and argued in the clubs, in tone and values the school was the school of the middle class girls. Yet whatever the pupils' background they had common problems and common delights in adolescence—ambivalent treatment from adults, difficulties in adjusting to other adolescents, new and exciting curiosities about themselves and the worlds they were beginning to see. The school offered them a sense of responsibility, or vocational ambition, of duty towards the nation as a whole. And these were good and important qualities, even if sometimes confusingly wrapped in outward forms of manners, decorum, restraint. The middle class girl could absorb the outer and inner form offered in this way. The working-class girl sometimes took or rejected the outer form. Some never perceived its centre, some only found it slowly and late. At school the stress, at its best, fell on qualities of individual living, on privacy, on social advancement, on emulation; and, much less noticeably, on winning access to the world of art, literature and music. The tension between the values and opportunities here, and those sketched in earlier chapters, ought to be a rich one, allowing the individual to realise himself in taking some of both. Or at least recognising them as possibilities of living. But it didn't work that way. Partly because both school and girls confused the unimportant surface codes of middle class life—what was 'respectable'—with the central qualities. Partly because crudely selective schooling of the grammar school type is inevitably based on too tight a relationship between social class and educational opportunity. Like all such schools this one tended to select, hold on to and value the middle-class child. So the working-class girls turned away from the school to the coffee bar, and thence by marriage into the upper reaches of working-class life. Neither working-class nor middle class life offered developed institutions to teenagers. For the teenager, it was a matter of building their own institutions almost from scratch—gathering under the clock, in the library, or in the park, going into pubs under-age or adopting a coffee bar. Looking back on working-class community from this distance, one begins to see how it becomes invisible—no more than smoky chimneys and cramped streets with people sitting on doorsteps.

Working-class Community

Before advancing further it might be worth looking at the key term in this discussion—community. Working-class community rests on the division of labour in society. The working-class family has few, if any, financial assets. The man has nothing to live from except his labour and his skill. His job is unlikely ever to give him enough money to build up capital, let alone employ others. His earnings probably reach their peak in his early twenties, and thereafter—except for trade booms—they will hold still, or decline. His chances of promotion from the shop floor are negligible. And though he may earn more or earn less than his neighbours, the range of income in a working-class area is very tiny compared with the range and forms of income amongst a middle-class group. Contrast this with the middle-class man whose income tends to rise through his life, who is usually on some promotion ladder, who may build up a small amount of capital, and who knows that many in the middle class might be ten, twenty, thirty times as rich as he is. This single economic division, whatever else it does, pulls the working class together as a group; and as a self-conscious group—whereas it splits the middle class into much more separate households, even if joined by common bonds of interest.

A second bond between income and community comes from the cycle of poverty that Rowntree classically analysed. Since income is low and little-changing, and capital negligible, the working-class home with young children is very much worse off than its neighbours. The child is born within the poverty band. This was very strikingly true earlier in the century. It is still true in the Britain of today. Children in working-class families, especially larger ones, are very badly off—and so are their parents. When the children reach working age, and are still living at home, this alters—since a teenage boy can often earn as much at an unskilled or semi-skilled job as his older, experienced father. Income is multiplied in a way not met with in middle class homes. For a brief period, there is uncharacteristic prosperity: the phase seized on by some to denounce families with large incomes living in subsidised council housing. It passes, and once the children leave home there begins the slow drop into the poverty band again. In middle age the risks of illness and accident increase, and without capital there are fewer cushioning devices to help the working-class couple. Finally retirement (which to a schoolteacher may mean purchasing a bungalow on the south coast), means the sharp and final drop to subsistence level. And as the man dies before his wife, for her it foreshadows a drop even below that. This deep and terrible rhythm is the very ground of working-class life. It works its less visible course even in the more prosperous present. It reminds the man that his family lives by his physical strength, and that in a narrow way not felt by the rest of society, his wage-earning burns up his physical body. No one in our society has a shorter life than he.

From it springs the shared and repeated experience of hard times together. Without money to fall back on, men must turn to each other for help. And out of that necessary habit of mutuality grow not only the friendly societies, the unions, the co-ops, but all those groupings of community described in the previous chapters. Those groupings are the tighter because income and work originally compel the working class to live in dominantly one-class neighbourhoods, and then the style of living evolved makes it more difficult to live—or want to live—in a more mixed district. But neighbourhood is not simply a geographical statement. Neighbourhood is based on a tight criss-cross of kinship patterns. The working-class family is less mobile, less 'national', than others. Their jobs, opportunities and aspirations make them stick to the local scene. A doctor might buy a practice anywhere in Britain—to a large extent he chooses roughly where he will live, and chooses nationally. A working-class man normally considers jobs in only one locality, and when he does move—like the Irish or the Scots—it is not from choice but from compulsion: there is no work at home. Not only is mobility restricted like this, but customarily the working man has less access to forms of long-distance communication. He does not have a telephone, and may be ill-at-ease using one. Coming from an oral society, and with a background over many generations of second-class education, he is not a letter writer. Even more intimate than these pressures towards building up and remaining in a neighbourhood, is the fact that the kinship pattern is based more on where mothers and daughters live than on what the menfolk might want to do. Daughter normally lives near mother, and though this has been taken as 'read' for the purposes of this study, it is basic to all discussions of community. The network of extended families may draw in individuals (an unmarried son stays at home, an old neighbour is adopted as an 'aunt'), and certainly binds the neighbourhood as a whole together.

Work, the old poverty cycle, neighbourhood, the extended family—this is the settled structure of community. In turn this structure leads to a style of living which again adds to the structure: for there is a further way of analysing working-class society. If the community is built up 'vertically' through kinship, where people of different ages—grandchild and great-aunt—are joined together; it is also built up 'horizontally' where people of the same age but different families are joined in a strong social bond. It begins in childhood. Boys and girls play together outside the home at an earlier age and with much less supervision than middle-class children. We know this is commonly misunderstood by less professional social workers who judge a mother neglectful when she is perfectly typical. Children lead an intensely social street life and park life, and it doesn't appear to cause harm. This continues up to and through teenage where the roving peer group is not in itself menacing, but is almost always treated as if it were by middle class observers or by the authorities. At the courting stage the working-class difference is evident again. Courting is done in groups. You'll see a group of girls in mid-evening pass a group of boys, exchange a few words and carry on. Yet at the very end of the evening the groups will meet again, break down into couples and the apparently casual exchange of words earlier on turns out to be between boys and girls who have already fixed their wedding day. Only at marriage does this pattern break, and then only briefly. The man is still among his mates all day at work, the woman builds up her daytime group of other women—relatives and neighbours. And very quickly this spreads into the evenings, so that the husband (again, a difficult judgment for the social worker) naturally spends many evenings out with other men of his age, and the woman has her similar body of friends, knitting, playing bingo, watching TV, around the home. What has to be recognised is not that this is bad or good, but that it is different and part of a larger logic. The whole style heightens that intense and continuous sociability which is one of the strongest impressions of working-class community.

At the other extreme is the lack of privacy. There isn't any privacy because the houses are so small, and only one or two rooms can be properly heated. The only place which is private in the way that a professional worker's 'study' might be, is the lavatory—unless you can retreat under the bedclothes early. The lavatory is the place that the man studies his wage chit, or the woman a new and daring purchase. But against this the home is the place of a very restricted sociability. Only relatives have the freedom of the home. The vision of the working-class home as ever-welcoming, kettle-on-the-hob masks a formidable code of manners. Neighbours who are not kin, are very careful about when they come in (never when the man is eating). General sociability only begins beyond the doorstep. The middle class visitor who uncomprehendingly breaks the rules is treated of course with the courteous tolerance that the Japanese extend to Americans breaking in on their tea ceremony.

A further strand, which you feel almost at once, is the episodic nature of life. Watch a working-class boy walk along one of his home streets—he taps on a window, rings a bicycle bell, picks up an orange at the grocers, throws it in the air and puts it back. In the pub he doesn't just order a pint, he asks the landlord if it's free beer tonight—he makes a tiny incident, and his path is a trail of minute happenings. It's as if the horizons of life are firm and immutable, and interest can come only from a series of lively kicks within the too-settled structure: vitality within fatalism. The extreme of this is the pull of crime—or more rarely, drugs—as 'incident'. But much more normal, and germane to this study is the pattern of language: the argument by anecdote, the jump from one vivid little story, compressed to an image, developed to a tale—to yet another—when a middle-class person would have turned either to abstract logic or perhaps to the deadwood of social diction.

Directness of the speaking voice is intimately related to community. As we can tell from the earlier chapters, working-class societies and clubs are far less specialist than they look. The brass band, the Labour party ward, the bowls club—are not so much the centre of a particular skill or interest as fields in which to develop and extend personal relationships. Because of this, and because of the clearly defined roles which people tend to occupy, the working-class man or woman—within his community—has the certainty, and sometimes the panache, of a Shakespearian actor on the Stratford stage. This certainty about who you are and what the world around is, this practice of acting out personal relationships, and the concrete, documentary habit of thought produce that 'directness' of speaking and that incipient metaphorical life which could be so rich a ground for any developed culture.

The deeply grained habit of co-operation, the habit of valuing people rather than concepts, and directness of emotional response are probably the main qualities that a civilised society should try to take over from working-class life. There are other values of course, and one negative is worth pondering. That is the surprising extent to which working-class life has been unaffected by the 'packaging values' of the new middle class style. The flimsiest side of the mass media, through cultural television programmes or colour supplements, has fairly easily penetrated middle class life. Working-class life, despite the fact that the working class is *the* mass audience, has held its ground more roughly.

But if we change the point of view, and look at community from the outside, we can see that there goes with it a suspicion of the new and strange which can be strong but can also be disabling. It is sceptical about the police, where the middle class is habitually romantic. It is sceptical about politicians, especially Labour ones. It is baffled by officials. It is ambivalent about deviants—sometimes there is the acting-out of dilemmas, as at the Jazz Club, sometimes there is the mutual problem solving within the family; just as often there are the unrecognised depressions ('she's just moody')—neurotic swearing in cold bedrooms. It is ambivalent about immigrants too. And even more so about the educated: the strong 'Jerusalem' strain in working-class life makes them value education as it makes them value political action—but just as they know that politicians feather their own nests, they also know that the educated use their gifts to exploit the uneducated as frequently as they do to serve them. Community ends very sharply, and if we are ever to develop its qualities for our whole society, we have to know not only whether it can exist apart from the cramped and unequal conditions that bred it, but whether it can be opened up to new experiences. By itself it has an important consolatory value in an unequal society, but it has little more.

Is it Going Anyway?

It is occasionally maintained that the working class no longer exists: 'We're all middle class now'. It is more commonly claimed —and perhaps the majority of professional people would support this—that the working class is now changing so rapidly that the concerns advanced in this book are of historical interest only. There have always been people who felt this. At any point over the last hundred years it was felt that an old working-class style of life was just disappearing: the English novel through Scott, Mrs. Gaskell, Dickens, George Eliot, Hardy, Lawrence, records with wonderful delicacy exactly such an impression in almost every decade. The truth is that working-class life has always been changing, but also that the relative economic position of that class has altered little. At certain times it may be poorer or richer, but it is always the base of the pyramid. This caution apart, it surely is true that working-class life is changing as speedily and more variously than it ever has been.

Perhaps it has changed most for the children. There are health visitors, clinics, new school buildings for some, school milk and school dinners. These are important, good physical health, such as other classes have enjoyed for decades, is a prerequisite for effective education—but more important are the experiences that they bring along with them. School has penetrated working-class life in two major ways. First, through play-centred teaching methods in the infants' school: sticking word-labels on objects in the classroom, learning elementary measures by playing with sand and water, discovering musical relationships by making simple instruments from biscuit tin drums to jam jars half-full of water. The middle class nursery always offered something like this: working-class community never did. And after good health and decent physical conditions, this fine pre-academic experience is essential if the great majority of children are to master the formal skills as successfully as children from more prosperous homes. But again a caution: most working-class children are still taught in very old buildings, in the largest classes our society tolerates, and —with honourable exceptions—by teachers who don't see the need or special importance of this child-centred approach to children who otherwise live in a strongly adult-centred home. Secondly, increased educational opportunity has opened up wider roads out of working-class life. Eighteen per cent of children from the upper working class reach grammar school, and eleven per cent from the lower working class.[1] Rather less than two per cent reach university, a figure which has not altered since the late 1920s.[2] But grammar schools and universities are overwhelmingly middle-class places, and the increased opportunities they have offered have largely gone to middle class children. The same applies to almost all the social services expanded or launched by the 'welfare state'. It is very easy to exaggerate the opportunities now offered to working-class children through education: they are better than they were, but they are disappointingly meagre. Nevertheless their growth means that working-class communities are more accustomed to the demands of school, and the old conflict between school and home may be in some ways less tense; though it is certainly—because of the complexity of education and the 'apartness' of teachers and administrators from those whom they serve—far more bewildering than it has ever been.[3]

No less important has been the effect on community of the new

[1] Douglas, J. W. B., *The Home and the School*, p. 154. The figures for upper middle class children were 54%, and for lower middle class 34%.

[2] *Higher Education* (the Robbins Report), 1963, Appendix Two (B), p. 4: 'There was little change between 1928-47 and 1961 in the proportion of students at university coming from working-class backgrounds in spite of the fact that the number of students at university had more than doubled during this period.'

[3] See March, L. and Abrams, S., *The Education Shop* (1966), for an analysis of why schools do not communicate effectively with working-class parents.

freedoms in women's lives. Families can be planned. The perpetual pregnancies and nappy years are now a much smaller proportion of their lives. From the age of thirty onwards it is
generally possible for mother to return to work in the mill or
the office. The tradition of domestic service in middle-class
households has shrunk, and women—ever since the factory
demands of the First World War—have been inside the men's
world of work. The change in the personal quality of women's
lives has surely been immense. Contraception removes fears about
love making, eats into that thick net of taboos built protectively
around working-class sex. Your children don't die. Neither do
you.[1] The plastics revolution removes almost intolerably hard
physical work from the home. And the demands of home are
easier to bear, knowing that there is the chance of working years—
with the social life, the skills, and the income they will bring.

But how does this affect working-class community? It certainly
alters the balance between home and community. The home is an
easier, more welcoming place for the man home from physically
hard, frequently monotonous work. It is no longer odd to see a
young husband pushing a pram. If at the same time an old
community breaks up through re-housing, there can be a strong
turning-in to the home. But I doubt whether by itself this destroys
that pattern of working-class sociability which I described as
'community'. It changes it. Outside the home couples do spend
more of their time together, within a larger group—such as a club.
But it is still a minority of time—a once a week, or end of evening
pattern. The other change is that the group of women—kin
groups or peer groups—who always made up the daytime life,
are now establishing themselves inside the old male worlds, like
the mills, the clubs, and even the unions. And without doubt I
would say that this brings an enrichment and not a diminution of
community.

Nevertheless, the most serious challenge to the old patterns has

---

[1] In 1889 infant mortality was 94 in 1,000 for the middle class and 247 in
1,000 for the working class. See Laslett, P. *The World we have Lost* for a
superb account of the effects of the continuing industrial revolution on
English life ('When Queen Victoria died at the very outset of the twentieth
century one person in four could expect to come to this—a solitary burial
from the workhouse, the poor law hospital, the lunatic asylum.')

been the enormous rehousing of the working class that our society has undertaken since 1945. The face of England changes faster in ten years now than it did in any previous hundred. We build between 300,000 and 400,000 new houses a year, a huge number of which are in council estates on city outskirts replacing the working-class districts near the centre. Almost all this work has been carried out in complete ignorance of the styles of living that I have been discussing. To take a typical example, the new towns were built on a fine ideal—that all classes should live in freely-mixed neighbourhoods. But the lack of social knowledge on the part of the decision-takers has meant that the population of the new towns is made up of skilled workers and their families, not the semi- and unskilled workers who needed the new conditions far more. It has produced a peculiarly shifting population because it is so difficult for married children to get a house near to their parents: each new generation is ejected from the town. Community centres are no substitute for community, and much needless unhappiness—especially that arising from deep feelings of not 'belonging'—could have been avoided. And finally, the classes have refused to live together: the managers move out to neighbouring villages, and the neighbourhoods voluntarily change into one-class districts without the depth and complexity of the older working-class communities. All this, as my first chapter indicated, has been established several times.[1] But of all the changes to the old style, this is the one that has most effect.

A more vivid change has come from the build-up of organised

---

[1] See especially Young, M. and Willmott, P. *Family and Kinship in East London.* Rehousing schemes, if crudely done, are certainly capable of wiping out slowly-grown communities; and by putting people in new homes with strange neighbours, can result in a more home-centred life, and one in which people attempt to settle their uncertain status by conspicuous buying of prams, lawn mowers, washing machines, cocktail cabinets, cars. But one unexpected result is that by lifting the common expectations of what every person in the street should possess, people are economically worse off than before. Increase in wages have not met the suddenly-raised minimum of decent living. Inevitably hire purchase and other debt-building arrangements exploit this market, so that far from being catapulted into middle class life, the rehoused worker is only more aware that what chiefly dictates his position is his relatively unchanged working-class income.

mass markets, and the growth of the mass media. Almost every-one shops sometimes at Marks and Spencer, almost everyone might have the same washing powder in their kitchen. Four million people might buy the *Daily Mirror* one morning, ten million might watch a big programme on ITV that evening. And because of this it has sometimes been argued that we are moving towards a new kind of 'classlessness'. But if the crucial element in class is income and work, it is hard to see how using the same mass products as people more prosperous and powerful than yourself breaks the class barriers. Certainly a large number of products from cigarettes to branded bacon are sold to all classes, and if you like are 'classless' objects. But it is not so cut and dried. To mention cigarettes immediately reminds us of the close and deliberate connection between particular brands and social status. And the merest glance at half-a-dozen of the major London stores —Harrods, Heals, Liberty's, Selfridges, John Lewis, C and A, tells you that they reflect, serve and perhaps reinforce quite different social groups. The signs are there not only in the price and kind of goods they offer, but in every detail down to the very lettering on the stalls. The mass market in goods has been almost wholly good to the working-class. It has lifted standards, reduced work and increased pleasure. Sometimes it has made us all own identical objects; more often it has led us to buy broadly similar goods within each social band. But it has not had anything to do with dissolving those bands.

A much stronger case than this might be made out for the effects not of the mass market but of the mass media. The argument here is that by offering experiences in common, and by operating from relatively standard scales of value, they begin to alter people's feelings and remould the old values. Certainly they do offer new experiences within the working-class community. The beneficial effects of television, for example, would be hard to over-rate. The more cramped the home, the more welcome it has been as relaxation, pleasure and amusement. And it brought into working-class homes (along no doubt with much inconsequential material) pictures, pleasure, information and ideas which were previously only open to more prosperous and educated people who were able to use books and theatres and travel abroad. It can't be denied that along with this has come a rather conventional set of homely values, selected so as not to offend. And behind these, in the *manner* of presentation, lie those 'packaging' values, which now patronise and now exploit, that have been developed by the highly-educated group who work in the worlds of television or journalism. I certainly don't think these do any good, and in the previous studies you sometimes note the sometimes bewildering gap between working men and women and the mass media which purports to reflect them. They may have some effect in standardising our responses, whatever background we come from. But I doubt if it is as great as is sometimes argued. Partly this is for the reasons I summarised in the first chapter—that the mass media are not so 'mass' at all, nor are we. They break down into programmes or papers aimed at distant and existing groups, and we of course, are in the end individuals who, given exactly the same stimulus, yet respond with incredible and unchartable variety. Perhaps the middle class has, rightly, always placed a special trust in the printed word because they know what it can transmit. This may have led to their over-emphasising the effects on individuals of standardised or debased language in newspapers, magazines, paper-backs. But I'm not so sure that either the printed word, the poster or the television screen have quite the same 'reality' for a working-class audience. Some believe, some don't, but I'd emphasise that if we look at these from the point of view of an enclosed, oral society rather than that of an educated and literate one, then the nature of their 'reality' may well be different. Certainly any working-class audience has a fairly strong degree of scepticism about politicians or pop stars—stories about Bing Crosby having to stick his ears back or Alan Ladd wearing high-heeled shoes to make him look tall, are part of everyday talk. A company can send out a standard programme or paper but individuals don't receive it in standard ways—we skip and select in mysteriously complex ways rising from the very depths of our individual personalities.[1]

One by one, checking through the forces that make for change, I think that whatever the true weighting may be, the idea that the working class is ceasing to exist in the old way: a submerged and

[1] An interesting American example of an Italian working-class community in Boston selecting from TV programmes is set out in Gans, H. *The Urban Villagers* (1962).

alternative culture based on habits of co-operation and values of community is false. The true report is probably a more untidy one, impossible to qualify and difficult to analyse. In most ways working class is undoubtedly far, far better than it was. But in essence it *feels* the same, offers the same kind of *experience*.

Chapter Eleven

SOME PROPOSALS

Why it Matters

And so the claim is not only that these questions of working-class community are of the present and the future, but that they matter a good deal too. They matter first of all, because in the purest way we should and must know ourselves. We know very little about the way most of our fellow citizens live, and why: less than we know about life on some South Sea islands. But only with that knowledge can we begin to comprehend possibilities of individual living, choices we could make, and the consequences for others of social decisions we support. Always one pleads for more research. Yet I doubt if our knowledge and understanding of common life in this country will be fully advanced by the social survey kind of research which has often been our characteristic mode. Most British research has sprung from immediate, utilitarian needs—the decision-makers requiring information on a major problem of the moment: divorce, delinquency, early leaving from school. Such survey research begins by being problem-centred, and almost certainly ends with proposals for administrative reform. Inevitably the picture it builds up is of working-class life as one set of problems, and of middle-class action as administrative change. It would be churlish not to point out that this line has been the distinctive British contribution, the source of most of our knowledge of our own social lives, and the impetus for countless changes which have made human life more bearable for huge numbers of people. To many people, sociology is almost synonymous with the social survey, as pursued by great figures of the past such as Seebohm Rowntree and Charles Booth, or a present master of the mode like Peter Townsend or Michael Young. Of course this is only a part of what we mean by sociology, and unfortunately one reaction—very common in the universities —has been to reject it, and treat the necessary work on the theoretical bases of the discipline as being not only 'pure' sociology, but sociology *tout court*. Probably the need to establish this new subject, to announce its academic credentials, both in American and British universities has exaggerated this division. Perhaps too, we are affected by the realisation that the old tradition of the lonely scholar, will partly give way to that broad front advance—loose teams of workers on a common question— which now characterises the physical sciences. Of course sociology must learn, as history has done, that a rich discipline not only can, but must contain diverse approaches: literary, utilitarian, theoretical.

And this is rather hopeful. Because what we need in order to understand working-class life better, is not only social surveys. We need pure—if you like, useless—research both from sociologists and anthropologists. We require not only the research worker who is motivated by a defined problem and the search for useful, administratively applicable knowledge. We also need the research worker who is simply curious, who wants to find out what working-class life is and how it all fits together. I doubt anyway if we are particularly good at telling in advance what is likely to be useful or not. Medical research surely teaches us that the great breakthroughs come at the most unexpected, most unforecasted points.

The knowledge this all might bring could help us progress to a more equal society. At the very least it would question the myths of affluence and continually reveal less visible forms of deprivation and hardship in working-class life. But it might do more. The progress need not only be from disadvantage to equality: it can be from disadvantage to difference. We would at least know the points where we might choose in favour of a more diverse society, where we would take over qualities from working-class life, as from other groups such as the new immigrants. There isn't much to be gained by rushing at the question head-on: can we transmit to the future valuable qualities in working-class life, without transmitting the inequality and disadvantage too? Surely the answer is that sometimes we can and sometimes we can't—it is likely to be a matter of many, many particular decisions, involving loss and gain in complex and untidy ways. But potentially there is diversity and there is gain. There are other qualities than those that flourish in middle class life, and they can be important ones not only socially—values of co-operation balancing values of emulation—but in terms of individual realisation too: Lawrence Lowry, Henry Moore, remind us of that.

The second broad reason why these questions matter, is that even if we can see the best social decisions to take, we can't take them effectively unless we know something about the way knowledge flows through our society—who communicates with whom and how. I'm particularly concerned about the decisions, service or advice offered to the working class by the immediate representatives of the middle class—teachers, doctors, ministers, city architects, social workers, librarians, managers. Their trouble is not that they don't want to help, nor is it their lack of experience —but it very often is lack of knowledge of the way information has to be filtered through unobtrusive leaders if it is to get inside primary groups within the working class. It must follow natural paths of communication which are as invisible to an outsider as a forest spoor to a tourist.

In the sociology of working-class life there is a tiny but intriguing suggestion in *Coal is Our Life*.[1] The researchers study life in and around a Featherstone colliery in Yorkshire. At the time, Britain badly needed to increase its coal output. Politicians exhorted miners to work harder, newspapers attacked 'absentee-ism', productivity posters and leaflets appeared everywhere, well-qualified men and women investigated 'the problem'. The effect of all this was very slight indeed. Just possibly there was no likely way of altering the miners' attitudes and increasing pro-ductivity. Certainly there was none at all, *unless* one seriously investigated the what and why of the miners' attitudes and those of their community. And that research would only get anywhere if it was pure, untrammelled by the problem, and at liberty to be simultaneously serious and useless. The team who wrote *Coal is Our Life* were not at all concerned to help the industry raise production: they were university lecturers studying in the field. And in their investigation of the colliery they considered all the

[1] *Coal is Our Life*, op. cit.

variables in the miners' lives. It was by doing this that they conceived the idea of a table, in one column of which they might list the number of tons mined, and in the other the results of Featherstone Rovers Rugby League Club. Suppose the two matched: then to understand why the miners worked harder one week than another, one had to bypass all the middle class productivity appeals and drives, and enquire a little more deeply into the miners as a community: the physical skill and mock combats of Featherstone Rovers in some way represented them as a group —as the grinning miners on the productivity posters certainly did not.

It is a minute example. But if we knew more than we do about, say, clubs in working-class communities, it is not improbable that we might come across knowledge which might—for instance— help us to overcome prejudice, and integrate immigrants (another example where too much of our energies go into exhortation), or help delinquents, or increase that kind of information or motivation in the home which gives the child a better chance of profiting from education at school.

What knowledge we do have of how we might communicate efficiently with working-class communities probably lies not with the teachers and city officials but with the politicians: at least those who note the vote-surveys which show people making up their own minds in ways not related to mass media propaganda or bias. Since the seminal[1] analysis of the Roosevelt election in 1948, other surveys have shown voters making up their mind at a family or primary group level, and not at a national one. People changed their votes because of personal contact, not because of what the papers, politicians or placards directly said. In some way the politicians' promises were filtered through opinion leaders in the primary groups. But it is only at unusual moments that politicians observe this fact. Most of the time their election campaigns are really based on a mistaken assumption about how the mass media communicate, and a great deal—if not most— election campaigning of this sort is probably quite irrelevant. Similarly in times of crisis during war, military intelligence has been forced to abandon what I have, rather loosely, called the

---

[1] Lazarsfeld, Berelson and Gaudet, *The People's Choice* (1948).

Some Proposals

middle class assumption about communication. During the 1939-45 war social scientists showed how German troops could be effectively persuaded only if military intelligence accepted that the ordinary soldiers had 'lead' figures in each group: to change these leaders' minds was to communicate with the whole group.[1] It is also probably true that advertisers, again at moments of crisis—for example when a Government bans tobacco advertising—question the 'middle-class assumption' and acknowledge that brand-buying is done not on the direct recommendation of the advertisement, but on the personal recommendation of a group or family leader—like mum. None of this adds up to much. It is only taken seriously in times of crisis. But compare it with a politician's or newspaper's reaction to a strike—where often enough you get a vivid example of exasperating non-communication, which press or politician rationalise by spotlighting or inventing organised cadres terrifying the 'moderate leadership'. A little knowledge of ordinary life in Britain might frequently lead to a much more fruitful analysis. But in no field is there less sense of this communication problem than in that of the face-to-face decision takers in the social services—from city planners to police inspectors and schoolteachers. Despite the fact that they are in immediate contact with the working-class community, so much of their dialogue gives the impression of middle class addressing middle class, with the rest only 'listening in'. Ironically, the same is true even of mass circulation newspapers and top-drawing television series.

Notes on Strategy

In this book I am defining a problem and suggesting its importance, and I haven't been concerned with advancing specific proposals. But without going that far, perhaps I could sketch the kind of strategy which might lead to practical help. I would begin with the universities. It would be an enormous advance if one university department of sociology was built up which

[1] See, for example, Shils, E. A. and Janowitz, M. 'Cohesion and Disintegration of the Wehrmacht in World War II', *Public Opinion Quarterly*, XII (1948), pp. 280-315; Dicks, H. V., *Psychological Foundations of the Wehrmacht* (1944). For similar findings in a study of the U.S. Air Force see Grinker, R. and Speigel, J., *Men under Stress* (1945).

modelled itself in some ways on the systematic pure research of a Medical Research Council unit, and in others on the strong, unimpeded relationship between pure and applied research that we see, for example, at the Department of Applied Economics at Cambridge. I suggest then that one university department of sociology should specialise on a long-term attempt to build up a Social Map of Britain. If it is true that we know more about life on some South Sea islands than we do of life in the English North, then the university department chosen would produce research report after research report which *systematically* reversed this. As the Oxford Dictionary stands to English linguistics, or the great Atlases to geography, so—over a period of several decades—the reports of this university would stand to our social knowledge of Britain. And of course, the research would be pure, not problem-centred. Such a university (there might be a special rightness about York or Liverpool), would have to have field stations—in Newcastle, Cardiff, Birmingham and so on—where research workers lived in the local community for spells. I have in mind the very good models of Toynbee Hall earlier this century, or the Institute of Community Studies now. But no small, independent unit like these could do the task I sketch. That requires long-term support, both from the University Grants Commission and the overall policy of the university concerned. And it requires that research workers, though encountering the communities under study, should spend a lot of their time back in the university, facing the stimulus and criticism that it alone can offer. So this would be the basic job: a social map of Britain.

As the map built up, the second line of strategy would be to contact people who needed immediate practical help. They would anyway, just as the doctors begin to link themselves to Medical Research Council work, or as politicians and industrialists demand to know more of the developing model of the economy being built at the Cambridge Department of Applied Economics. A good precedent here are the refresher courses offered to probation officers and to almoners by some university departments of Social Administration—like that under Professor Titmuss at London or under Professor Townsend at Essex. So, a second university should have to develop a Department of Applied Sociology. The Department of Applied Sociology should run a coherent series of courses for the people who meet the problems face to face—doctors, teachers, planners. This would give it a different feel from the questions from that offered by the pure research workers. Then the Department should establish its own series of problem—answering research projects—whether into delinquency, or violence, or education, or redundancy, or what. Again these would have to be systematic and fairly specialised. But they would have three vital qualities that most social research now lacks. First, they would draw on the Map of Britain, and have a sense of normality that we do not yet possess. And that map, like pure research in biochemistry or nuclear physics, might at this stage produce its most unexpected practical results. Second, they would build one on another: not a series of unrelated projects, depending upon individual interests here and there. This policy control should lead to finer quality, and wouldn't affect the other kind of once-only research conducted elsewhere. Thirdly, they would have an editorial sense of who they were serving. They would not be addressed to fellow researchers—as almost all social science projects are—but to those doctors and planners and such whom the Department knew through its courses.

As a third line of development, a good paperback publisher like Penguins should now be brought into the strategy, just as the Nuffield Science researches linked at the crucial stage with the publishing firm of Longmans. The publishers would strengthen this editorial sense of a particular audience needing precise help. We know that relatively few teachers or council officials would read the Map of Britain reports, and again the audience for the reports from the Department of Applied Sociology, though much larger, would still be small. The paperback publisher therefore, would initiate a series not of general topic reports, but of precise ones each aimed at a distinct decision taker—*Sociology and the Planner, Sociology and the Teacher, Sociology and the Doctor, Sociology and the Hospital.*

That would be a general strategy stemming from one university department. But there are other lines that could be started at the same time. For example, the Social Science Research Council could sponsor a more short-range and more adventurous plan. It could mount a series of *operational research* projects. Each of these would be aimed at a different subject—industry, school, medical care, immigrants, the old. Each would take the problem of communication, and try to show how it could be met by beginning with the natural lines of communication in working-class life. A good precedent was the *Education Shop*[1] project, where instead of trying to communicate with elusive parents only by sending out terminal reports, or inviting them to open days, information was got to them and children's difficulties eased by putting it across their shopping track in the local Co-op. This reversal of the normal could be tried in each subject by the Social Science Research Council. Instead of doing little more about immigrants and integration than letting a Bishop urge us on, a deliberate experiment could be set up in a chosen city. Two lines (there are others) might be tried. One would be to test the assumption that there is a leadership group in working-class life who quietly organise most of the communal activities, and who very strongly influence the rest of the community. That tiny group could be defined, could be won over to the idea of integration, and per-suaded to help—perhaps by introducing coloured immigrants into closed groups, like union branches, or working men's clubs, or choirs, or angling clubs. The hope would be that by an intense attempt to change this leadership group you changed the com-munity. Another line would be to look more closely at sport in working-class life and the prestige it confers. It may be that coloured workers instead of being despised, feared or rejected, would be more admired and sought after if they were manifestly excellent at an activity the community valued. In sport, this might be something unexpected—not cricket, tennis, or football, but pigeon racing or billiards. You can't be sure, but it would be worth testing whether a series of successful coloured teams in different sports altered the entire valuation of the immigrant by the surrounding communities. But of course, I'm only hinting at a strategy. And all that can be done here is to point up the problem of the relationship of working-class and middle class life, and insist that we needn't, even if sympathetic, stand helplessly by.

The third broad reason why the questions raised in these studies matters is this. Britain was the world's first industrial nation. That change to industrialisation—and to different forms

---

[1] See March, L. and Abrams, S. *The Education Shop*, op. cit.

of industrialisation, from steam power to computer—is still going on. Every other country, in some degree, will have to face the problems we have met.[1] All of them must meet, in an industrial context, the problems of community and belonging, of choice or ascription, of diversity as well as equality. Our domestic problem of how to question middle class values and how to scrutinise and bring into play the working-class strengths are problems of all post-industrial societies. We are the test station. We gave the world the mechanical basis for industrial life; we could give the lead in the quality of living possible within the new urban life.

I don't know how typical Huddersfield is. But so far as I can see much even of the detail could come just as easily from life in Sheffield, Newcastle or Leicester. In Wales, Scotland, London and the South, the voices would change, the institutions too— pigeon lofts or chapels might crystallise the interlocking strands of community where I've used clubs or bowling greens. But even there I think the salient features, etched in different detail, are very similar. I know that in order to concentrate on other points I have used working class and middle class as if there wasn't within each an immense diversity. But allowing for this, the working-class qualities remain tenacious in a more affluent era, and being bred by the common conditions of the industrial revolution they are found the length and breadth of the land. The fact that industrial workers over ten generations made so much out of such squalor and indignity remains one of the little miracles of British social history.

Yet this achievement, this style of living is substantially sealed off. There is, of course, the old wall of values which has often prevented important sections of the middle class from seeing, hearing, and respecting the differences, as opposed to the dis-advantages, of working-class life. Curiously, the age of the mass media with its huge audiences overlaying the old class boundaries, also has not really brought working-class life on to the public level—the plane of recorded existence. Instead it has more characteristically produced a series of packaged imitations which are not 'a mirror held up to nature' nor meant to be so: they are

---

[1] 'English social experience since the death of Victoria is the only lengthy experience any country has ever had of really mature industrialization'— Laslett, P. *The World we have Lost* (1965), p. 205.

images which retain the maximum, and substantially, working-class audience, by meeting the demands of our most common and inconsequential fantasies. Similarly, one might expect large numbers of working-class children who pass into middle class citizenship through the education system, to bring with them the more valuable qualities of working-class life. To some extent they do, but the main drift is the other way—the gifted working-class girl or boy may blank out, ignore or reject his background. In Britain, the closed society of the centre is extraordinarily supple in narrowing down or even avoiding the new open roads that our age brings or emphasises. None of this is an *individual's* work—no teacher or reporter or television producer deliberately acts so as to blot out the style of living I discuss. What I describe is the consequence of their attitudes and actions as groups: elites re-adjusting themselves, as technology or the economy opens up fresh forms of communication and of social mobility.

One could very well argue that a country like India, despite its rampant poverty and suffering has an incredible treasure to yield if the industrial age was entered on not with a sense of wiping out the past, nor, heaven help us, with a folk-museum sense either—but with an openness about its not being wholly bad. Such an attitude, expressed in the million and one decisions of policy and action, is the scaffolding that is needed.

But the attitude will only come the more that working-class life (and similarly the life of Lagos and Calcutta) is brought into public recognition. In Britain our knowledge of our own society is extraordinarily literary in basis. Yet our literature of all kinds from the novel to mothercraft manuals is very strongly a middle-class literature. And as I've argued previously, the new kinds of public statement in the mass media remain paradoxically middle-class too. Our view of Britain still has these limited horizons. That's one reason why direct social mixing—sharing the same school or the same doctor—is important. And why, through novel, film, research, or television, we need to hear, and to see all the voices and all the faces.

None of this suggests that we shouldn't end under-privilege and the ignorance and suffering and stunting it causes. *That* is paramount. Where there is a choice between maintaining in-equality or preserving some special feature of working-class life, we must surely forgo the second. Inevitably, much must be lost. Nor do I suggest we fix on a romantic working-class past. The life is there now. It's good and it's bad. We need to know how and why. There is always the tension—a clash between two goods —the need for equality and the desire for diversity. In a society like India's the drive for equality must be relentless. But in Britain we can perhaps add to that—if only we have the experience and the data—a concern for diversity, and the strengths that middle class life can't easily give our civilisation. It would be hard if in the social engineering—education systems, welfare, rehousing, central and local government, communications—which is very properly our concern, we overlooked the unexpected bounty from the wretched industrial past. What men have slowly made—and wonderfully too—out of squalid conditions deserves cautious and imaginative use.

INDEX

Index